RELENTLESS
COURAGE

WINNING THE BATTLE
AGAINST FRONTLINE TRAUMA

EARLY REVIEWS

"From the first words, I was all in. The story went straight to my core. As I write this the tears are welling up in my eyes, not because of my own trauma, but because I am so happy and thankful that the two of you wrote this book for us. This manuscript review opportunity has already made such a difference for me personally in my lifelong struggles that come with working as a first responder. If your story can elicit this response from me, think of how many other first responders you can reach, before they get to the edge of that cliff. I want to thank you Mike for having the courage to come back from some very dark places that I have also been to, and ⸹ sharing your very private thoughts, feelings and raw emotions which hopefully will be understood by many people. Doc, I would also like to thank you and tell you that without the work you have done, many more of us would no longer be walking these streets. Your work is very important, and your message is clear."

Lt. Shelly James
Walnut Creek Police Department (Retired)

"*RELENTLESS COURAGE* has break-through potential for guiding leadership within the law enforcement community. There is a big difference between leading an organization and leading a Tribe and *RELENTLESS COURAGE* is the first book I've read that identified this difference. Every leader in the LEO community needs to read this book, and then rethink their role in changing the culture. Reading *RELENTLESS COURAGE* was like taking a walk next to Michael Sugrue as he brings you deep into his own journey. His courage in sharing his personal experiences is truly relatable and will be life changing for others who read this book. Doc Springer's analysis and insights were delivered in a down-to-earth, totally relatable way. Reading her portions of the book felt like sitting on the back porch with Doc and learning a range of new ways of thinking about trauma and healing for first responders. Both Doc and Michael showed the human side of trauma and its impact - the way they shared his story and identified psychological insights related to it was uniquely powerful - I've never seen this kind of format before, and it is very effective."

Chief John Carli
Vacaville Police Department (Retired)

"In *RELENTLESS COURAGE,* police technical know-how collides with clinical expertise to tell a story of trauma, despair, hope, and healing. If Michael can heal from his injuries, so can you! Unbelievably brave, every American needs to hear this story! Doc Springer and Michael Sugrue have moved the officer wellness conversation a decade into the future."

Chris Littrell
Police Officer, Police1 Columnist and host of the Gravity Podcast

"I have been a police officer for more than 23 years. I worked motors, SWAT, CSI and was a trainer at numerous Police Departments and the Police Academy. I have served for 16 years on the board of the Police Union and I've been its President for a decade. I have worked multiple traumatic events including numerous homicides, suicides, as well as personally being involved in 3 on-duty shootings. I have been injured in the line of duty requiring surgery. The work that Michael Sugrue and Doc Springer are doing is saving lives every day. And their new book? To make an ice hockey comparison, their book *RELENTLESS COURAGE* is the game-winning goal in game 7 of the Stanley Cup."

Ron Bruckert
Retired Police Officer and POA President

"*RELENTLESS COURAGE* takes you deep into First Responder trauma and the damage and despair associated with it. But along with this, hope, healing strategies, and coping mechanisms are brought to light. As someone who has survived child abuse, cancer, multiple heart surgeries, head trauma and negotiated with several hundred individuals contemplating suicide from the Golden Gate Bridge, I have observed and been through a fair amount of trauma. This book is a game changer for me, and a must read for any First Responder."

Sergeant Kevin Briggs
California Highway Patrol (Retired) and Author of Guardian of the Golden Gate

"*RELENTLESS COURAGE: Winning the Battle Against Frontline Trauma* is an unapologetic hard hitting and necessary read for all public safety and military leaders. Our frontline responders deal with significant daily trauma. Doc Springer and Sgt. Sugrue do a fantastic job clearly articulating and translating these issues into teachable moments for those who selflessly serve our communities and for those that lead them. Ten Stars all the way around!

Dave Weiner
Chief of Police (Retired), US Department of Veterans Affairs, and United States Air Force Veteran

"We don't have to sacrifice our heroes to atone for our cultural failings. We don't move forward by denying our wounds. In *RELENTLESS COURAGE,* we are allowed to bear witness to the trauma our first responders carry in our name. I recommend that if you live in America, you should prioritize this book. Our warriors and first responders are carrying the traumatic weight of our nation that we cannot endure without them. If we blame first responders and ignore their traumas for political or ideological prestige, we do so at a high cost to our nation's health and honor."

Magnus Johnson
Former Green Beret and Founder of Mission 22

"Understanding the traumas that Law Enforcement Officers face throughout their careers and the long-term effects that those traumas have in their lives is exceedingly difficult to both describe and comprehend. That is why this book is so important. When you read the perspectives from the police point of view by Michael Sugrue and then from Doc Springer and her professional experience, you can truly grasp the pain of our police experience. This is an important work as it creates a pathway to healing."

Lt Randy Sutton (Ret)
34-year police veteran, Author of A Cops Life and Founder of www.thewoundedblue.org

"*RELENTLESS COURAGE* takes you on a journey while taking a very unique path. The expertise of Doc Springer, combined with the vulnerability of Sergeant Mike Sugrue, bares strength and courage in bringing these difficult conversations out of the shadows and into the open. Their tireless work will change outcomes and needs to be shared at all levels of an organization, from preparing our recruits entering the profession to developing much-needed, trauma-informed leaders."

Chief Neil H. Gang
Pinole Police Department, Member of the Board of Directors for the California Police Chiefs Association

"*RELENTLESS COURAGE:* Winning the Battle Against Frontline Trauma provides invaluable insights into the experience of police work and how to heal from frontline trauma. Doc Springer walks with Michael Sugrue through his trauma journey, gently cracking open the door and sharing her insights, and together they expose, with measured care, what is rarely seen by those outside of police work. Throughout the book, Michael Sugrue smashes the stigma through his vulnerability, providing a roadmap for others on the frontline who are on similar journeys. As a specialist who focuses on police trauma and wellness, I highly recommend this easy-to-read guide on winning the battle against frontline trauma."

Jason M. Palamara
NYC Police Department Cold Case Homicide Detective (Retired) and U.S. Navy Veteran

"Leadership is influencing others in order to get results. Plain and simple. Too often, law enforcement leaders concern themselves with current crime trends and diminishing budgets instead of the mental health of their team. Life is often messy and as law enforcement professionals, we all have a front row seat, which takes a toll on us. Michael's experiences coupled with Dr. Springer's professional knowledge, should serve as our wakeup call. Michael's dedication to bettering the lives of those who have struggled as he has is incredibly noble. I am honored to call Michael a friend and brother."

Aaron Fuller
Chief of Police, Knoxville, IA Police Department and host of the Leadership in Law Enforcement Podcast

"*RELENTLESS COURAGE* is an essential read for all first responders and their families. Michael Sugrue's vivid description of his traumatic journey provides the reader with a stronger understanding and insight into the lasting impact of critical incidents. Dr. Springer does an outstanding job eloquently breaking down Michael's experiences from a clinical perspective. Her analysis offers a deeper layer of knowledge and awareness to those experiencing symptoms of PTSI and helps those surrounding them to better understand their plight as they endeavor to provide their support. *RELENTLESS COURAGE* is an excellent collaboration that will definitely have an impact on all who read it."

Lt. Steve Bertolozzi
Walnut Creek Police Department (Retired)

"I'm extremely grateful to Sergeant Mike Sugrue (Retired) and Dr. Shauna Springer for their detailed work on *RELENTLESS COURAGE*. In recent years, Mike and Shauna have pioneered a new way of looking at First Responder trauma that sadly, has been largely ignored and dismissed over the years. I strongly suggest public safety and military leaders take the time to not just read, but to embrace Mike and Shauna's experiences and thought-provoking analysis. Make this book a cornerstone of your leadership style, openly discuss it with your organizations and develop a culture of care for your organizations, and their family members, to benefit from."

Ryan J. Millay
Lt Col, USAF (Retired)

"*RELENTLESS COURAGE: Winning the Battle Against Frontline Trauma* is a wakeup call for commanders, supervisors and leaders. The stigma of seeking help still permeates the ranks of our civilian and military first responders. Our missions are directly impacted by our inability to identify those suffering from trauma, seek help, manage expectations of our superiors and put these warriors back on the line. We'll make our communities safer, our directives and missions more successful, and heal our tribes from within. This work is a toolkit that must be used and will directly impact the health of our first responders and the perception of policing today."

Benjamin R. Jacobson
Lt Col, USAF (Retired)

"*RELENTLESS COURAGE* is a must read! Sgt. Sugrue and Doc Springer have produced lessons learned for all - from the patrol officer to the Chief of Police! Sugrue and Springer clearly describe the true effects of an Officer Involved Shooting, with critical analysis and key insights throughout. Recognizing the demons in front of and inside of us is something we all need to better understand. Learn how you can help yourself and do it with support! *RELENTLESS COURAGE* is an open door inviting you in, don't pass it up!"

Dan Hartwig
Retired Deputy Chief, BART Police Department

"RELENTLESS COURAGE is a must read for any Law Enforcement Officer or First Responder. The stories told through the heart of Retired Sergeant Michael Sugrue are horrifying and encouraging at the same time. HEALING IS POSSIBLE if you are willing to speak up and speak out. As Law Enforcement Officers, we cannot avoid or control the trauma we face, but we can control how we react and cope with it. Shauna "DOC" Springer explains how the mind works through trauma and gives us all hope that we can heal. I want to personally thank both Sergeant Michael Sugrue and Doc Springer for teaming up to tell such a difficult story and provide ways to heal. This book will save lives!!

Lieutenant Sean Conley
Walnut Creek Police Department (Retired)

"While this country battles its way through a mental health crisis, Doc Springer's books, *WARRIOR* and now *RELENTLESS COURAGE,* peel back the curtain surrounding trauma in our military and law enforcement worlds in a relatable context. In *RELENTLESS COURAGE,* former Air Force officer and police Sergeant Michael Sugrue walks us through the stages of trauma throughout his career, showing that the stigma against mental health exacerbates the healing process. When we know better, we do better...this book is worth the read!"

Lt. Col. Angela Jacobson
United States Air Force (Retired)

"*RELENTLESS COURAGE* is a book that we all desperately need right now, and it couldn't have come a moment too soon. Our nation's LEOs are in crisis, and there is no civilian psychologist out there who knows the warrior's heart like Doc Springer does. Michael Sugrue has lived a police officer's worst nightmare, and his courageous sharing of his story, paired with Doc Springer's expert unpacking of its psychological underpinnings, provides a multifaceted and unprecedented look into the heart of the complex traumas that America's police officers are privately suffering. This should be considered essential reading for anyone in the law enforcement community, anyone concerned with officer resilience, and those seeking real understanding of--and solutions to--the suicide epidemic among LEOs in our country."

Alice Atalanta, Ph.D.
Author specializing in work with the Special Operations community, and founder of the SOFxLE program--bringing resilience solutions from members of SOF to LEOs nationwide. www.sofxle.com

"RELENTLESS COURAGE is a MUST READ for all persons involved in any emergency response work, including police officers, firefighters, and paramedics. This book should be required reading for all first responders, from the newest hire to the highest levels of department leadership, to include all administrative and elected officials with civilian oversight of emergency response departments. I had the honor of serving with Sergeant Mike Sugrue for over 10 years while employed as a Patrol Sergeant and Watch Commander Lieutenant with Walnut Creek Police Department. Mike was an outstanding police officer with unlimited potential. Mike's forthright sharing of his personal experiences and Doc Springer's insightful analysis is a winning combination. Doc Springer shares her wealth of knowledge in easy-to-understand terms that are very helpful to the reader. I highly recommend that this book be prescribed reading in all entry level academies and revisited during advanced officer and in service training. Having served in a combat zone as a Marine Corps Officer, I can personally attest to the unseen trauma that takes its toll on the bravest of the brave."

Timothy J. Barrett
Lieutenant Colonel USMC (Ret.), Lieutenant Walnut Police Department (Ret.)

"Mike Sugrue bares his soul to the world with excellent insight and analysis from Doctor Springer. Together, they are helping save lives with this book."

Chief Joel Bryden
Walnut Creek Police Department (Retired)

RELENTLESS COURAGE

WINNING THE BATTLE AGAINST FRONTLINE TRAUMA

Michael Sugrue and Shauna 'Doc' Springer, Ph.D.

 HIDDEN IVY PRESS

(San Francisco, CA)

RELENTLESS COURAGE: Winning the Battle Against Frontline Trauma

Copyright 2022 by Michael Sugrue and Shauna 'Doc' Springer, Ph.D.

Cover design by Daniel Sundahl, based on photography by Tori Lee

For further information, visit www.docshaunaspringer.com.

Publisher's note:

This publication is designed to provide insights about first responder trauma. Reading this book is not a replacement for professional therapy. There are many high-quality resources listed in the appendix of this book. If the support of a licensed therapist is needed, readers are urged to get this support from a culturally competent professional who understands the kinds of insights that are shared within this book.

Library of Congress Control Number: 2022902768

ISBN: 978-1-7368244-1-2

DEDICATION

I dedicate this to Mike Gormley, my hero, my protector, my dad.

—Michael Sugrue

I dedicate this work to those who risk it all to protect and defend all of us, even when society does not protect and defend them in return, because being a Protector and Defender is who they are, in their deepest heart and soul.

—Doc Springer

Foreword to
RELENTLESS COURAGE
by Michael Sugrue and Shauna 'Doc' Springer, Ph.D.

By Lt. Col. Dave Grossman

RELENTLESS COURAGE is one of the most important books of our time. Building on her previous book, *WARRIOR: How to Support Those Who Protect Us,* 'Doc' Springer has teamed with Michael Sugrue to give us the vital, essential, "next step forward" in *understanding and healing* the trauma inflicted upon our first responders in these tragic, violent times.

In order to recognize how profoundly important and essential this book is, you need to understand some critical concepts.

First, consider the fact that we assess the level of violence in our society by the murder rate. The "number of dead bodies" is how we judge the severity of violent crime and the magnitude of the overall problem. *And that measure is profoundly flawed.* When we look deeper, we will see that the situation is much, much worse than it looks.

Medical Technology is Holding Down the Murder Rate

We must understand that the *murder rate under-represents the level of violence,* because *medical technology is saving even more lives.*

In 2002, Anthony Harris and a team of scholars from the University of Massachusetts and Harvard, published their landmark research in the journal *Homicide Studies.* They concluded that advances in medical technology between 1960 and 1999, *cut the murder rate to a third, or a quarter, of what it would otherwise be.* And the leaps and bounds of life-saving technology in the decades since then, has had a similar impact in saving the lives of even more victims of violence. Thus "preventing" even more murders. Therefore, you must multiply homicides in the 1960s by a factor of about 3.5 to compare with the 1990s. And a similar dynamic is in play between the 1990s and the 2020s.

Everyone understands the concept of "inflation adjusted dollars."
When we finally start reporting "medically-adjusted murders" then
we will begin to appreciate just how desperately, tragically *bad* the
situation has become. For every murder we report, *there are ever
increasing numbers of our citizens* physically maimed and scarred,
and emotionally crippled and traumatized by violence. *And* we
must also consider the trauma inflicted upon the "responders" who
were "there for them" in their hour of need!

Because of life-saving lessons learned in two decades of war, today
virtually all "responders" (police, EMS, and firefighters) use
tourniquets to save lives, every day. Some medical experts believe
that tourniquets alone may have cut the murder rate in half in just
the last decade. Today almost all police officers carry tourniquets,
while twenty years ago this was unheard of. If a responder slaps on
a tourniquet and saves a crime victim's life: they have prevented
a murder.

And that is just one small aspect of the astounding medical
technology being applied every day, holding down the body count
and saving lives. But also concealing just how violent and
destructive our nation has become.

(There is a temptation to use "aggravated assault" data instead of murder data, but it is too easy to "fudge the figures" on "ag assault." Any seasoned old cop will tell you that we can make the ag assault rate say whatever we want it to say, by shifting that "magic line" between ag assault and "simple assault," very much like "grade inflation" in our schools. Murder, however, is solid data. Dead is dead, and it is hard to "fudge" those numbers. But to use murder rates over any period of time, we must allow for medical technology, just like allowing for inflation when comparing minimum wages across time.)

The annual increase in homicides in 2020 was 30%. The worst we have ever seen previously is a 12% annual increase in the 1960s. But that comparison between 2020 and the 60s completely breaks down! You must multiply homicides today by a factor of about seven -- and that is a conservative estimate -- to compare with the 60s! What happened in 2020 is at least 20 *times worse than anything we have ever seen before. And 2021 is even worse: compound interest, stacked on top of 2020!*

When we look at police officers murdered in the line of duty, we must consider the impact of this medical revolution in saving cops' lives every day. But with police we must also look at ever-evolving factors such as body armor, tactics, TASERs, backup officers, and countless other lifesaving dynamics constantly being brought into play.

Our "first responders" are "out there" in these violent times, and the great paradox is that their amazing lifesaving skills are saving the lives of vast numbers of our citizens, and thereby "reducing" the murder rate. These "responders" are immersed – indeed, they are virtually "marinated" -- in this toxic realm, doing their job and saving lives: 24/7. 365. Every day. In every city and every corner of our civilization. And the great paradox, the enormous irony is that the reduction in murder that they achieve, makes us under-measure and under-appreciate the magnitude of the problem and the enormity of the trauma that they endure daily!

The Psychological Trauma of Violence

There is another important dynamic that we must consider. A monstrous mass murder by a single individual can create more psychosocial trauma than countless deaths by disease. In its section on PTSD, the DSM-5 (the "bible" of psychology and psychiatry) tells us that, whenever the cause of trauma is "human in nature" (such as assault, torture, or rape) the degree of trauma is usually "more severe and long lasting."

Millions die from disease every day and it has little impact on our behavior. But one serial killer or serial rapist can paralyze a city. And one horrendous mass murder can stun a nation.

Thus, the over all societal harm of violent crime can be far greater than the harm caused by disease or other deaths by "natural causes." And *this* is the toxic, corrosive, psychologically destructive *sewer* that we ask our responders to work in, every day, everywhere.

In particular, this book captures the "sense of abandonment and betrayal" felt in the aftermath of this tsunami of trauma experienced by our police. And the critical point is well and truly made, that "these trends will get increasingly worse until we collectively remember that the police are a vital part of our society."

In *On Killing,* I document the fact that our returning Vietnam veterans were spit on and verbally attacked. It really did happen. And now, as Michael and Doc point out, "we have done the same thing to our LEO professionals as we did to our Vietnam veterans." The authors have summoned the intellectual foundation and the moral courage to assert that we must do "the hard work of weeding out those who abuse their power," and we must look "at the ways *we ourselves need to change and grow.*"

This is the clarion call to action, in support of our police, who are striving to follow the path of the protector:

> "They do their *human best* to judge situations and
> motivations with the goal of keeping us safe...We
> need to have their back, in the same way that we
> support our warfighters...
>
> Specifically, we need to ensure that our first
> responders have truly safe places where they can
> directly address their trauma. We need to make sure
> they have access to trusted Docs and trained peers.
> We also need to look at treating the biological
> symptoms that create injuries to their nervous system.
> Addressing these things will change the entire
> equation when they are working on the streets."

In the face of this challenge – as is so very well put – we must
accept that "evil is real" and "embrace the fullness of our own
humanity" to lead us home from a realm of evil, into a future of
healing, compassion, and *love*.

Relentless Love

RELENTLESS COURAGE could just as easily have been entitled,
"RELENTLESS LOVE."

The Bible says, "Greater love has no one than this: that they *give* their lives for their friends" (John 15:13). To which I would add: there are many ways to *give* your life. Sometimes the greatest love is not to sacrifice your life, but to live a life of sacrifice.

Looking again at John 15:13, it is worth noting that many people *will die* for their friends. Audie Murphy was the most decorated American Soldier in World War II. When asked why he did it, his answer was, "They were killing my friends."

Thus, a lot of people will die for their friends. But what kind of person will die for strangers? What manner of love is this: that they will go out the door every day, going in harm's way, and putting their life on the line *for people they don't even know?*

In *On Killing* I wrote about how medical personnel in combat draw their strength and courage in a unique manner, motivated from a powerful drive to protect. Not just medical personnel, but all peacetime, civilian responders are *always* trying to save lives.

Police officers use "deadly force" when they sincerely believe *there is no other option to prevent an immediate threat of loss of life, limb, or grievous bodily harm.* When a police officer must shoot someone, the moment that individual is no longer a threat, the cop will call an ambulance, leap on the body and slap on a tourniquet, or apply

CPR and other first aid, to save that person's life.

This poem then, applies to all our nonmilitary peacetime responders:

> But they take not their courage from anger
>
> That blinds the hot being;
>
> They take not their pity from weakness;
>
> Tender, yet seeing.
>
> They endure to have eyes of the watcher
>
> In hell and not swerve
>
> For an hour from the faith that they follow,
>
> The light that they serve.
>
> This light, in the tiger mad welter,
>
> They serve and they save.
>
> What song shall be worthy to sing them
>
> Braver than the brave?
>
> --"The Healers" by Laurence Binyon
> World War I veteran

The opposite of evil is not good. The opposite of evil is *love,* because evil is the absence of love. Love defeats evil, as light banishes the darkness. And our first responders truly embody the sacrificial love that Jesus was talking about in John 15:13. Indeed, the source of their "relentless courage" can be found in 1 John 4:18: "Perfect love casts out fear."

Thus, an important note must be made here. The most amazing thing is that the vast majority of our responders *do not* get PTSD. We must not create a self-fulfilling expectation that they will all get PTSD.

But more and more of them *do* need our help. Too often the "trauma tattoos itself onto [their] retinas and plays itself out in grotesque private movies." And *when they do need our assistance,* the model set by Michael Sugrue and Doc Springer, to "smash the stigma" and help those who "look in the face of evil," is the standard by which such assistance can be modeled and measured!

Because: "We have lost too many of our Protectors and Defenders, fallen by their own hand because they suffered in silence, and then died in one final act of desperation."

The Natural Successor to On Combat

In my book *On Combat* (with a half-a-million copies sold in five languages, Google Scholar says it has been cited in academic publications over 600 times) I introduced a standard by which we can understand and assist those who have encountered the toxic realm of combat.

In *On Combat* I talk about memory gaps (as is so very well narrated in this book, with Doc Springer's amazing gift of "listening eloquently"), *and* memory distortion, tunnel vision, auditory exclusion, slow-motion time, and many other "normal" responses to combat, which would otherwise meet every definition of a psychotic episode! Thus, during 2020, in the height of the pandemic, *On Combat* was Amazon's number one best seller in multiple medical categories, as the book was embraced by the medical community in the midst of that astoundingly traumatic, demanding, tragic event.

Doc Springer and Michael Sugrue have now taken the lessons in my book and given us a quantum leap forward in this essential realm. Thus, *Relentless Courage* is truly the natural and essential successor to *On Combat*.

For Such a Time as This

A virus of violence, a cancer of crime is exploding in our streets and in our lives. This explosion of violence and mass murder is real, and this is the psychologically toxic and corrosive *sewer* that we ask our responders to operate in -- always just a phone call away! -- to save our lives and the lives of our loved ones. Our responders sustain our civilization, but who will sustain them? Their relentless courage and compassion must be matched by an equally relentless determination to sustain and support them, and *that* is the critical task so well and truly embodied in this book.

Thus, I implore you to read and heed this book! I believe that Michael Sugrue and Doc Springer, and their book *RELENTLESS COURAGE*, was put here (as it says in the Bible, in the Book of Esther) "for such a time as this."

With all my heart I encourage you to read, study, and apply this book, so that you can help save the lives of those who save our lives, and join Michael and Doc in leading us home from the dark and tragic place to which we have travelled.

Lt. Col. Dave Grossman (US Army, ret.), author of *On Killing, On Combat, On Spiritual Combat, and Assassination Generation.*

Bio

LT. COL. DAVE GROSSMAN, U.S. Army (ret.)
Director, Killology Research Group
www.killology.com

Lt. Col. Dave Grossman is an award-winning author, and nationally recognized as a powerful, dynamic speaker. He has authored over a dozen books, to include his "perennial bestseller" *On Killing* and a *New York Times* best-selling book co-authored with Glenn Beck. His books are "required" or "recommended" reading in all four branches of the US Armed Forces, and in federal and local law enforcement academies nationwide.

He is a US Army Ranger, a paratrooper, a prior service sergeant, and a former West Point Psychology Professor. He has five patents to his name, has earned a Black Belt in Hojutsu (the martial art of the firearm), and has been inducted into the USA Martial Arts Hall of Fame.

His research was cited by the President of the United States in a national address, he has testified before the U.S. Senate, the U.S. Congress, and numerous state legislatures, and he has been invited to the White House on two occasions to brief the President and the Vice President in his areas of expertise.

Since his retirement from the US Army in 1998, he has been on the road over 200 days a year, for over 24 years, as one of our nation's leading trainers for military, law enforcement, mental health providers, and school safety organizations. He has been inducted as a "Life Diplomate" by the American Board for Certification in Homeland Security, and a "Life Member" of the American College of Forensic Examiners Institute.

TABLE OF CONTENTS

EARLY REVIEWS V

DEDICATION XV

FOREWORD... XVII

ACKNOWLEDGMENTS 1

FIRST RESPONDERS ARE TRAUMA RESPONDERS 3

OUR UNIQUE WAY TO TELL THE STORY.................................. 7

PREFACE: THE RAVENS 15

Chapter 1: THE DEEP CUT OF TRAUMA 25

Chapter 2: TRIAL BY FIRE... 39

Chapter 3: NEAR DEATH EXPERIENCE................................... 55

Chapter 4: STING... 69

Chapter 5: SOLITARY CONFINEMENT 87

Chapter 6: ACCUSED...105

Chapter 7: ATTACKED..119

Chapter 8: MY DAD 147

Chapter 9: RECKLESS PURSUIT 165

Chapter 10: WAKEUP CALL..185

Chapter 11: THE BEGINNING OF HOPE.................................203

Chapter 12: A CAREER-ENDING BETRAYAL.............................223

Chapter 13: LAST DAY 249

Chapter 14: HEALING 269

THE FUTURE OF LAW ENFORCEMENT....................................294

About us..325

ACKNOWLEDGMENTS

This book was made for the first responder Tribe, with contributions from many within the Tribe.

We are honored that Lt. Col. Dave Grossman supported us with such a moving foreword for our book.

The cover design from Daniel Sundahl perfectly captures the feel of first responder trauma and the mental warfare that ensues. Daniel is an incredibly talented artist, firefighter and paramedic who draws from his own experiences to create spellbinding work.

(See more of Daniel's work on www.dansunphotos.com)

Tori Lee, a retired Sacramento, CA police officer, is the

photographer of the image of Joe Deorian, a Richmond, CA police officer, that Daniel used to create the cover design.

We deeply appreciate those who came alongside us and contributed stories, suggestions, edits, and statements of support, including John Davison, Noah Blechman, Magnus Johnson, Ryan Millay, Tom Gormley, Chris Littrell, Andrew Smith, John Carli, Dan Hartwig, Ron Bruckert, Donna Forman, Jesse Ney, Shelly James, Angela Jacobson, Ben Jacobson, Sean Conley, Steve Bertolozzi, Tim Barrett, Neil Gang, Randy Sutton, Dave Weiner, Jason Palamara, Alice Atalanta, Al Molien, Rodger Ruge, Jeff McGreevy, Kevin Briggs, Joel Bryden, and Aaron Fuller.

FIRST RESPONDERS ARE TRAUMA RESPONDERS

First responders are called to support us on the worst days of our lives. They respond to and are impacted by many traumas as part of their work.

They see and hear things that are burned into their memories forever – things most of us can't even imagine.

They see the worst in humanity and then they go home and do their best to be a loving partner, parent, and friend.

In a sample of more than 700 police officers from three major police departments, on both the east and west coast,

About a quarter...
- Have seen a fellow officer be killed or injured in the line

of duty (23%)

About a third...

- Have been exposed to a badly beaten child (35.9%)
- Have personally been seriously injured, intentionally (23%)

Around 40%...

- Have been exposed to a sexually assaulted child (40.6%)
- Have personally been shot at (38.1%)
- Have been trapped in a life-threatening situation (39.4%)
- Have had to make a death notification (42.1%)

Over half...

- Have been threatened with a gun (50.8%)
- Have been threatened with a knife or other weapon (55.2%)

Nearly all...

- Have seen someone dying (87.2%)[1]

Here are some additional statistics to consider...

---

1   Weiss, D. S., Brunet, A., Best, S. R., Metzler, T. J., Liberman, A., Pole, N., Fagan, J. A., & Marmar, C. R. (2010). Frequency and severity approaches to indexing exposure to trauma: the Critical Incident History Questionnaire for police officers. *Journal of traumatic stress, 23*(6), 734–743. https://doi.org/10.1002/jts.20576

- More officers die by suicide each year than are killed in the line of duty, by all causes (including "felonious" and "accidental" deaths, other than those where COVID was the cause of death)[2].
- Nationwide, the risk of suicide among police officers is 54 percent greater than among American workers in general[3].

We are losing good men and women, whose collective trauma, never addressed in an effective way, becomes too heavy a burden to carry. The impact of this trauma deserves to be recognized and addressed.

2   Sourced 12/8/21 at: https://www.washingtonpost.com/local/death-by-suicide-among-police-is-a-quiet-epidemic-it-needs-to-be-acknowl-edged/2021/08/09/c7dc2036-f941-11eb-9c0e-97e29906a970_story.html

https://datastudio.google.com/u/0/reporting/45630efa-3ee8-4c8f-ab44-ccbe-743f0b53/page/Kh2dC
3   Sourced 12/8/21 from: https://www.policeforum.org/assets/PreventOffi-cerSuicide.pdf

OUR UNIQUE WAY TO TELL THE STORY

It all started with a simple conversation. Michael shared his story with me. After I got over my surprise that I knew none of this, even though I lived within 10 miles of where each of his traumas had happened, I asked him, "Have you ever considered writing this up for a book?"

Michael said he had given it some brief thought, but the main block was that he hates writing. He told me he had written so many police reports in his life that he didn't want to do a lengthy writing project.

And that was the end of that conversation.

But Michael's story didn't dissolve and fade into the pool of trauma stories I have heard over many years as a trauma psychologist. Michael's story kept bubbling up in my mind.

A couple months after our first conversation, I went back to Michael. I told him that I really enjoy writing and felt that his story should be shared. Together, we figured out a unique way to tell the story.

First we would decide on the focus of each chapter. Then we would schedule a zoom meeting. I would listen very carefully to everything he shared about that topic. At first, I recorded these sessions and used a program that translated Michael's words from our zoom meeting into a word document. This formed the basis for the initial draft of the first couple of chapters.

But something about this process made me a feel a little "boxed in." I have spent my career listening to people share their most important personal stories. The system I thought would help me share his story accurately actually blocked me from really leaning in and listening to what Michael was saying *and* what he was feeling as he spoke. So, I decided to try a different approach and just forget about the transcription program.

The goal here was not to simply record what he shared with me word for word. Michael and I were not aiming to write up a polished series of official police reports based on the traumas Michael had encountered as a police sergeant. For this to be successful, I needed to go beneath his words and walk within the emotional terrain of his experience. The real challenge was to 'listen eloquently' to what he was saying - between the lines - to accurately convey the deeper emotional significance and relational context of his experiences.

To write up the first part of each chapter, almost as if I were an actor assuming a role, I would step into Michael's story and voice and tell the story from his perspective. As soon as we dropped the use of the transcription program, we got immediate feedback from a trusted reader, Chris Littrell, who is a respected member of the LEO community, that the writing felt much more "alive." Our direction was clear from that point on.

After writing up Michael's portion of the chapter, I then switched into my own voice and shared my reflections as a trauma psychologist and trusted "Doc" within the military and first responder communities. As I wrote about in my previous book, *WARRIOR: How to Support Those Who Protect Us*, there is a fundamental difference between a "Doctor" and a "Doc" within the warrior tribes.

A "doctor" is a person with a higher degree and expertise that is recognized in the academic community. This is the default term used for providers with advanced degrees in systems where veterans and first responders receive treatment. However, in the military and first responder communities, calling a provider "doc" often connotes a special kind of trust. The heart of this distinction lies in the role the provider assumes with his or her patients. As a highly trained Special Forces medic once explained to me when he conferred the name of "Doc" on me, "Doc" is what soldiers call a trusted medic in their combat unit. He said there were three sources of medical care in the Special Forces: licensed MDs (referred to as "Sir"), medics who were unproven (called "medics"), and finally, the ones who could treat and heal other soldiers (called "doc") because "help was guaranteed when it was needed most."

The distinction goes beyond competence to the way each provider approaches his or her patients, and the nature of the work. Doctors are the identified "experts" who offer "treatments" to their patients. The core belief of a doctor is this: *Working with Warriors is my job. I use my education and training to offer treatment to help them recover.* For docs, trust outranks rank in the healing relationship. Instead of engaging warriors in a "one-up, one-down" treatment relationship, docs collaborate with those they support in a relationship of mutual respect. The core belief of a doc is this: *Working with warriors is my calling. I want to get better and better at this over time.*

Across the field of mental health care, countless people have exposed their most vulnerable experiences in therapy sessions, only to leave those sessions wondering what their psychologist *really* thought. This is because "doctors" of psychology are often trained to believe that an effective healing relationship involves one-sided disclosures only. Michael and I wondered, "What kind of insights could our readers gain if I showed them how a doc thinks?"

Although this was not therapy, and Michael and I are friends and collaborators, our goal was to give this book the emotional depth that is critical for all healing journeys. And then to pair this with transparent feedback and psychological insights from me, about the impact of trauma and how we heal. So, each chapter takes the reader deep into Michael's mind, in a raw and visceral way, and then brings the reader into my mind, as I identify key insights and universal truths within Michael's story.

Each time I drafted a chapter from Michael's voice, I would email it to him and ask him to give me blunt feedback. I asked him to not pull any punches so that I could make sure I captured not just the

story, but the emotional undercurrents that coursed below
the surface.

Most of the time Michael felt that what was captured was "spot on
and very accurate." But there was a chapter or two that needed
further work. In one case, he asked me if I was bored while I was
writing the chapter because he felt it had "dragged" a bit. This was
an important moment in our collaboration because it signaled to
me that Michael was not afraid to give me truthful feedback. If I
hadn't received this kind of feedback from Michael, I would've been
left wondering if I had captured the other chapters in the way that I
had hoped to.

I admitted to Michael that he was right - I was bored while writing
that chapter. Most of the time, writing these stories had felt
effortless. Most of the chapters in the book took a couple hours to
write, once I had taken the time to listen, and enter into the story in
my mind. But this chapter Michael noticed as "dragging" had been
a walk through the mud on my side. We went back to it with fresh
eyes and reworked it until we were both happy with it.

In the early part of the book, by design, I kept my voice relatively
small in proportion to Michael's. My goal was to encourage readers
to get to know Michael and really invest their attention in his story.

As our trust in each other grew and we moved toward the part of his story where Michael began to heal, my reflections started to take up more space.

For the most part, in my reflections, I stayed objective, and wrote them from my understanding as a trauma psychologist. However, it was important to me to avoid doing this from a safe place of clinical reserve. As I wrote in my previous book, *WARRIOR: How to Support Those Who Protect Us,* if we are to help people heal from the trauma, we must embrace the fullness of our own humanity, and balance this with our professional expertise as healers. This is what it means to be a Doc.

In fact, in one chapter, I felt moved to personally back Michael up when he said that he had lost memory of part of the night of his greatest trauma. Unless this has happened to you personally, it is hard to understand how this can happen. So, in addition to citing the research on how trauma-related memory loss *does indeed happen,* I drew from my own personal experience as well. I also lost part of the memory of a freezing cold night in Boston in an alleyway next to a college bar during an attempted assault. But that's a story for a later chapter.

If Michael and I accomplished the goals we set for ourselves at the start of this project, you as a reader, will gain a new perspective on the trauma that our first responders face. Even if you are a first responder yourself, our hope is that you will gain critical new insights and recognize the commonality between your experience and that of other first responders, even if the specific trauma events are different.

We hope to "smash the stigma" as Michael often puts it. Stigma is deadly. We have lost too many of our Protectors and Defenders, fallen by their own hand because they suffered in silence, and then died in one final act of desperation.

With the right insights and the right support, healing is possible. Michael and I talk about some of the treatments and programs that may be game changing for those who are suffering. At the end of the book, we included a resources section to help you get started on your own healing journey.

But first, let's get into the story.

—Doc Springer and Michael Sugrue

PREFACE: THE RAVENS

True or False: The Blue Angels are a team of stunt pilots that do air shows to demonstrate the capabilities of the U.S. Air Force.

Many people would say "True!" yet this is False. The Blue Angels program is run by the U.S. Navy to show the flight capabilities of Naval Aviators (think of people like Tom Cruise's character in "Top Gun"). In the same way, each military branch has crossover capabilities into what we often associate with other branches of service. The U.S. Marine Corps has an aviation component, and large aviation training facilities. And within the Air Force, there are certain Airmen who are selected to receive specialized training, including grueling use of force training, and cross-cultural communication.

They operate with nearly complete autonomy to secure U.S. aircraft and personnel, and through their actions, they discreetly avert international incidents. These professionals played a critical role during the withdrawal from Afghanistan, the largest non-combatant evacuation airlift in United States history. Between August 16th and September 11th, 2021, these Airmen directly secured Hamid Karzai International Airport in Kabul, Afghanistan, protecting and safely transporting more than 124,000 people as part of Operation Allies Refuge[4].

This elite group of Airmen are called "Phoenix Ravens." Since the program began in 1997, slightly more than 3,000 service members have earned the distinction of being added to their ranks. Every USAF Security Forces Member who flies with a U.S. President or Vice President must successfully complete Raven training. Each Phoenix Raven is awarded a number and credentials that are unique – and that number is never issued again. Michael Sugrue is

---

4   Leidholm, N. (2021, Oct 29). 436 Airlift Wing Public Affairs. "Dover AFB Ravens reflect on OAR (Operation Allies Refuge)." Accessed online: https://www.amc.af.mil/News/Article-Display/Article/2834650/dover-afb-ravens-reflect-on-oar/

number 1173.

What do the Ravens do? To understand the role they play, it's important to know that the Air Force maintains different kinds of bases, and these range depending on the types of missions they support. Certain USAF bases are aligned under what is known as the Air Mobility Command.

Travis Air Force Base in Northern California, established during World War II, is a good example of an Air Mobility Command base. Travis AFB has been a hub for flying troops in and out of deployments to war. If you ask a Vietnam Veteran where they first landed back on American soil, there's a good chance they will say "Travis Air Force Base."

The C-5s are massive planes often deployed by the Air Force Reserve that can carry other planes inside of them, or, if the mission calls for it, several firetrucks, a few battle tanks or a couple Black Hawk helicopters. These huge planes fly in and out of Air Mobility Command bases, along with a full contingency of tankers and refuelers – billions of dollars' worth of equipment. Someone needs to protect it. That's where the Phoenix Ravens come in.

The Ravens also lead autonomous teams that establish and protect expeditionary locations where the Air Force may temporarily operate. Structured similarly to their civilian counterparts, the Federal Air Marshals, they also accompany aircraft full of military personnel, civilian contractors and valuable equipment. In other words, they are a highly trained, adaptable security team that protects planes full of people and millions of dollars of military equipment, to prevent sabotage, destruction, or compromise. When they are in safe locations, such as Air Mobility Command bases within the United States, they are often identifiable on the airfield, because only Ravens and USAF Combat Weather and Pararescue Airmen are permitted to wear a flight suit and a beret. When they deploy to dangerous locations to protect or establish remote bases, they often work as part of a team that includes pilots, logisticians, and engineers. Many Ravens are deployed for 3-4 months out of a given year, and for those based in AMC units, they may be away from home for 7-8 months a year. In these missions, Ravens are often in plain clothes, foregoing uniforms to de-escalate tensions. Whether in plain clothes or in uniform, Ravens' main objective is to secure U.S. aircraft while parked on international soil, even if they have to put their lives on the line to secure the aircraft and the air crew.

As soon as Michael Sugrue heard about the existence of the Ravens, he wanted to be a part of this specialized team. In 2003, he was the highest-ranking Security Forces member in the group. Michael wanted to be tested to his fullest capabilities and felt that he needed to prove himself as a leader. Getting a chance to attend the Phoenix Ravens Qualification Course requires a result in the high 90s on multiple rigorous physical fitness tests that were originally developed by the Army. All Phoenix Raven candidates are thoroughly screened for the course by their Squadron Commander, who carefully evaluates past performance and determines suitability for potential service in a combat zone or during a humanitarian crisis. Ravens are initially trained at Fort Dix in New Jersey. The training, an intensive 22-day, 12-hour-a-day course, is both mental and physical.

Academically, they learn anti-terrorism and force protection, weapon system security, legal considerations, embassy operations, airfield survey techniques, explosive ordnance awareness, comprehensive aircraft searches, cross-cultural communication, and verbal judo, which is a "communication tool designed to generate voluntary compliance.[5]" On the physical side, they receive most of their training in a facility known to them as "The House of

---

5 Source: https://airman.dodlive.mil/2016/05/02/house-of-pain/They learn how to read the land for areas of potential weakness to attack.

Pain" where they vigorously exercise and train until they are slipping on their own sweat. When the program first started, it was called the "IHOP" as in "The International House of Pain" because Raven candidates came from around the globe for the training. Michael lost twenty pounds over the course of his training. Ravens receive training in combatives and ground fighting, the use of batons and other non-lethal weapons, and a variety of American and foreign firearms. Using frozen paintballs, which can do real damage, trainees engage in high stakes combat scenarios. Using paint balls exposes Raven candidates to sudden, startling pain and teaches them to hold onto their weapons and maintain their will to fight, regardless of the outcome.

The final test of their training is to prevail an assault by a group of six instructors, who are wearing "Red Man Suits", fully padded bodysuits to prevent unrecoverable injury to the instructors. A friend of Michael's, Andrew Smith, who was Raven #73, served as a Raven instructor for over a decade. As an instructor, he often lost more than 5 lbs. in a single day of training, while engaged in hours of hand-to-hand combat in a padded suit that was like a "walking sauna." Even with the suits on, the instructors feel the pain and come out of training sessions with black and blue legs. "The students find every place where the suits have less padding, for instance at the creases behind the knees where they bend, and they strike those places repeatedly with hollow batons that are designed to be disabling.

The trainees, who are not wearing suits themselves, must withstand intense periods of fighting, sometimes with multiple instructors, without giving up, even when they're injured. A fellow Raven was knocked unconscious just before Michael's final test. Michael's final engagement resulted in two cracked ribs. He said, "I couldn't breathe without pain for about two months, but you just don't complain. There's a reason they need to test us like this, and I understood it. They need to see how we would respond in an austere location with no back up force available. Anyone who gives up cannot do the job of a Raven." With a smile in his voice, Andy Smith said that he thinks he may have trained Michael during his final year as an instructor, but his memory isn't clear. Andy's joke became clear when Michael said to me, "Next time you talk to Andy, tell him that he sure did train me. In fact, he was the guy that cracked my ribs!"

While this kind of training can seem extreme, it's important to remember that the Ravens are often the only defense in the kinetic, chaotic and potentially violent situations where Ravens serve.

Becoming Raven number 1173 was Michael's proudest accomplishment during his time in the military. As the Chief of Security Forces for the 615th Air Mobility Operations Group, he was also assigned as a member of a GMAT (a "Global Mobility Assessment Team"). As part of this assignment, he was deployed along with a small team to do recon and assess locations that might be used as temporary U.S. air bases, sometimes in very dangerous, remote locations. Michael recalls flying into a jungle in the middle of Colombia during the peak of the drug wars. To give perspective on how dangerous this area was, in 2003, a plane that was part of a counter-drug operation crashed near the spot where Michael and his team were deployed, carrying five people, four U.S. citizens and one Colombian intelligence officer. The pilot and the Colombian intelligence officer were immediately shot and killed by FARC (the "Revolutionary Armed Forces of Colombia"). The three U.S. military defense contractors were kidnapped and held hostage by FARC for over five years, until their release in 2008[6].

---

6   Forsyth, J. (2008 July 3). Reuters. "Freed American hostages in 'good condition'". Accessed online: https://www.reuters.com/article/us-co-lombia-hostages-americans/freed-american-hostages-in-good-condi-tion-idUSN0341320820080704

Michael and a small team of operators went in to survey the area for a potential base – one that would be used by both the military and the DEA (Drug Enforcement Agency). As he explains, "There were only 4 of us. We landed in a barren airfield surrounded by a dense jungle. We were undercover, in plain clothes, and I had a concealed M9 Beretta on my body, and a broken down M4 rifle in my backpack."

For a couple of weeks, under the continual possibility of hostile action, Michael and his small advance team surveyed the surrounding areas, looking for where an attack was most likely. They drew up plans for base defense – for example, where to put fences, where to create defensive fighting positions, and where to place the most powerful weapons to protect this remote base.

This is the kind of work that Michael did in the Air Force. This is the kind of warrior that he is. But the story that follows is about a different kind of courage – one that is harder for many warriors than the courage it takes to face a physical threat.

Michael and I took our time to come up with the right title for this book. In the end we decided on "RELENTLESS COURAGE." This felt right because the courage it takes to overcome the acute stress and frontline trauma faced by many first responders may be a greater challenge than operating as part of a specialized team in our nation's military.

Confronting mental warfare is part of the warrior's path – whether a warrior is in the military or serving as a first responder. Michael has served in both communities – first as a Phoenix Raven in the U.S. Air Force, and then as a police sergeant in his post-military career. This is the story of how Michael found the courage to overcome a nearly lethal battle with mental warfare. This is the story of how relentless courage can help us win the battle against trauma.

1

THE DEEP CUT OF TRAUMA

A traumatic event that lasts a few minutes can change our entire future. There are days in our lives that rip time into two pieces – cleaving our past from our future - leaving a jagged, wounded edge that can propel us into a dangerous spiral. Thursday, December 27, 2012, was that day in Michael's life…

To begin the story, Michael invites us to ride along with him on the day that changed his entire life - and ultimately brought him to the center of his purpose.

***

It's Wednesday, December 26, 2012, the day after Christmas, I wake up late in the afternoon after my night shift, excited, thinking to myself how amazing my life is. We've recently moved into our dream home, and my marriage is everything I hoped it would be.

My beautiful daughter – just two and a half years old – giggling at me from her high-chair, is my everything. As a recently promoted sergeant in the Walnut Creek Police Department, for eight years, I have held a job I cherish as much as my family. This life is what I've always wanted – a job I love and a close-knit family, all of us in great health and optimistic about our future. I'm driving into work and I'm already making plans for the weekend. This is my Friday.

It's quiet on the streets – a few cars slide by. All the businesses are closed. No calls coming out – the radio is silent. All of us are in a relaxed and happy mood.

We decide to sneak just over the border of our patrol route at 2 a.m. to go to our favorite hamburger joint in the next town over. Normally I eat healthy, but the feeling of the coming vacation has settled in - I pig out, ordering a bacon cheeseburger, fries and a Dr. Pepper.

After our middle-of-the-night meal, I'm sitting alone in my patrol car, working on some reports. The radio has been dead silent for nearly two hours.

Suddenly, the squawk of a radio alert tone cuts through the silence – the sound reserved for the most serious calls. I've never heard the dispatcher's voice – or anyone's voice – sound this panicked.

"Calling all units! There is a woman barricaded inside a residence by a subject armed with a knife - Creekside Drive!"

I throw my binder to the side, put my lights and sirens on, and start driving as fast as I can. Thoughts are racing through my head - envisioning what I may face when I arrive. The short drive, lasting just a few minutes, seems like an eternity.

Again, the voice of dispatcher – panicked.

"There's a woman and a man now barricaded in the room."

I'm confused. Is there only one assailant with a knife or is there a third party in play?

I pull my patrol car onto Creekside Drive.

Nothing.

Silence.

It's extremely dark. I don't see any people. I'm looking frantically for the exact address. I see the address for the condominium complex, but I still don't know where the actual unit is located.

Again, the dispatcher. She's frantic, screaming on the radio: "Units! Units! There's a struggle! There's a struggle!"

And then she says that the line went dead. She's lost all communication with the people in the condo.

Blood-curdling screams cut through the silence - a female voice – the feral sound of someone being killed. Chills go up my spine and the hair stands up on the back of my neck.

My partner arrives in her patrol car. Thank God. I have back up.

We don't need words to communicate. I pull my gun out and I look at her and we just know - we start running...towards the direction of the screams.

It goes dead silent again – from blood-curdling screams to total silence. I don't hear anything. I don't see anybody.

We announce ourselves: "POLICE! COME OUT, SHOW US YOUR HANDS!"

Nothing.

Silence.

To the left of the front door, there is a full-length louvered glass window. My partner wordlessly motions towards the window. It's completely shattered into the condominium. Without hesitation, we give each other a nod and my partner goes in first through the broken window. I'm right behind her. My adrenaline is pumping. I'm super focused - scanning the area. All of my senses are on high alert; every sound, smell, sight, as I scan the area.

It's completely quiet. There are no obvious signs of a struggle. We have our guns out. We're looking up the stairwell and again, we're giving commands: "COME OUT, COME OUT AND SHOW US YOUR HANDS!"

Nothing.

Half a face and body appear around the corner at the top of the stairs. He's looking right at me - eyes wide open and glazed over. He's sweating profusely - staring straight through us. He's totally focused, unblinking.

I'm shouting commands. I'm telling him to show us his hands. He has a knife with a blue hilt - I can see it in his right hand.

It doesn't make sense. I've never seen a blue knife like this before.

My partner is yelling: "DROP THE KNIFE! DROP THE KNIFE!"

My adrenaline is pumping – and my vision is laser focused. I can see the glint of the blade.

I've never seen anything like it, my entire career, whether it be the military or law enforcement. In my mind, I'm thinking, "Why aren't you responding? Why aren't you listening? Why aren't you reacting? My gun is pointed right at you. I'm yelling at you as loud as I can that if you don't drop the knife, I'm going to shoot you. I am going to shoot you." With a sense of increasing dread, I'm thinking, "I don't want to shoot you."

And then he comes at us.

The walls start to close in, forming a tunnel vision on the threat as his arm comes up and he lunges at us with a stabbing motion. I can see the tip of the knife.

I shoot. He hurtles past us, down the stairwell. He's laying at the bottom, but I can't see any wounds.

I can see a large butcher knife in his hand and I'm still yelling: "DROP THE KNIFE! DROP THE KNIFE!" He rises and turns back towards us, coming back up with the knife in his hand and immediately I fire my weapon again.

Then silence. From complete chaos to sudden silence.

Eerily silent. Blood begins to seep across the floor. There is a void in his face where one of his eyes was previously.

It's obvious. He's dead. His wounds are absolutely devastating. I had an officer check his vitals and there was no sign of life. We immediately notified dispatch to have staging medical enter the condominium.

The couple emerges from the bedroom. The man is in shock, with no expression on his face. The female is crying – she looks shattered.

I walk outside and lose it. I sob with an intensity that only comes when people lose a loved one. I just lost a piece of myself. I can't believe this just happened, but it did.

I have to take control of the situation. There's no one else coming. I'm in charge.

A voice in my head, from years of training, says "Pull your head out of your ass. Get your shit together."

I do. I start giving commands, controlling the crime scene.

When medical arrives, I feel a huge sense of relief. I'm hoping they can save him, but I know he's gone.

As I arrive back at the police station, I have the feeling that I don't want to meet the eyes of my fellow officers. I sense that they are looking at me in a weird way. I feel self-conscious, wondering, "Why are these people looking at me like this? Why is everybody staring at me?" I feel like I'm in a fishbowl.

Eventually, I get brought up to a room. Someone I don't know comes to me and says, "We need to get your uniform and your gun belt."

I'm escorted to the locker room by a reserve officer. I've barely talked to this guy and now he's watching me get undressed. I feel like they are treating me like I'm a criminal.

They place my gun, duty belt, and uniform in evidence bags, as if I've just committed a crime. This doesn't feel right.

Next they take pictures of me. They ask me to put my hands out, to turn my hands over while they take photographs of them. I think, "This is what I do to criminals. Why are they doing this to me?

Why are these people taking my photos?

Why are they checking my hands?

Are they thinking I did something wrong?

Or are they wondering, did I mess up?

Did I commit a crime here?

It's hard to explain, but it doesn't feel right."

Doc Springer's Reflections

The fatal shooting of December 27 has been the central defining trauma in Michael's life. It is not his only trauma by any means – in the chapters to come, we'll hear about some of the other traumatic events that have been part of his service history. But it's the one that altered the course of Michael's life.

A traumatic event that transpires over a few terrifying moments can leave us locked in a state of helplessness and horror for many years. Trauma tattoos itself onto our retinas and plays itself out in grotesque private movies – disrupting our sleep, leaving us agitated and exhausted at the same time. Those who suffer from trauma that is not addressed can become suicidal. When we do not receive the support we need, we can begin to feel that Post-Traumatic Stress is a life sentence. For many of the warriors I've supported, this feeling of trauma as a "life sentence" is paired with a vague feeling of being morally tainted – in just the ways Michael is describing.

Trauma and moral injury are not the same thing. Trauma is an event which shatters our assumptions that the world is basically a safe place, and that others can be trusted. Moral injury is more personal – moral injuries directly alter our sense of self – making us feel morally compromised – like a "criminal" in a way that's hard to describe.

Those in the healing professions initially described "moral injury" as the shame that results from participation in acts or events that violate someone's sense of morality. The classic examples are participation in atrocities of war or mistakes made in the fog of war.

Moral injury then evolved to mean not only the commission of acts deemed immoral to the self but also helplessness to act in ways that are aligned with personally held values. The classic examples in this case are helplessly witnessing the death of a battle buddy or innocent noncombatants.

However, anchoring moral injury to acts of commission and omission misses the vast majority of shame-inducing experiences reported by the warriors – like Michael – that I've worked with and held in friendship. Moral injuries are not always caused by a discrete act or event and in many cases, they *don't require that warriors do something outside of their moral code.* In other words, we can be "morally injured" in a variety of scenarios that are beyond our control – even a self-defense situation like Michael's experience on December 27.

Interventions that attempt to highlight the officer's lack of culpability often do not stick. In other words, people who suffer from moral injuries may understand that logically, a situation is not their fault. They may nod their heads in agreement if a therapist makes this point. Yet, understanding and agreeing with the logic of this lack of culpability is a catch-22. If it's not their fault, then they have to reckon directly with the loss of power, the loss of control they might feel at the cellular level—which can be overwhelmingly terrifying.

Moral injury is a wound that cuts very deep. Successful treatment must be provided with thoughtfulness and care.

What Michael and I understand is that with the right insights and support, trauma, and moral injury, can be overcome. Healing after trauma is possible, as you will see in the chapters that come. This is a story of hope, but like all stories of hope, we have to walk through some valleys first to ascend to the place where hope lives.

2

TRIAL BY FIRE

Warning: The content in this chapter includes graphic details of traumas sustained by Michael, which are commonly experienced by those who serve in first responder roles. These memories may be triggering to some who have been exposed to trauma. Our purpose is to raise awareness of the level of trauma exposure that many of our first responders sustain as part of the work they do.

This chapter takes us to Michael's first couple of weeks on the job as part of the Walnut Creek Police Department. Walnut Creek is considered one of the most desirable places to live in the Bay Area. The downtown district is lined with trees that have sparkling white lights on them all year round. The area is known for its great schools, open spaces, and civic facilities, including an arts district area and endless options for high-end shopping. Surrounded by beautiful mountains, and sitting within an easy commute of San Francisco, it's a great place to raise a family while working in the city.

Walnut Creek averages 1-2 homicides a year, and historically, the crime profile has been similar to that of college towns in the Midwest – the most common crimes being bike thefts, valuables stolen out of unlocked cars and things like that.

***

The first phase of the job for a rookie police officer is field training.

During field training, if a call comes in that seems over the top, you are going to it. You need to get exposed to high-stakes calls, while you have support. That way, when you're cut loose as a solo officer, you won't be going through that kind of call without experience to draw upon.

On my first or second week, I had two calls that I'll never forget.

These calls were my introduction into police work in a city like Walnut Creek where everyone thinks, "nothing ever really happens in Walnut Creek."

These are not stories that I've ever brought up in any of my therapy sessions. They are not traumatic to me in that way, but I will never forget them, and certain things can bring these memories right back to me.

The first call was to respond after a fire at a condominium near the downtown district.

When the call came in, no one was really sure what happened. All we knew was that supposedly there was an elderly lady that lived there with her daughter and son-in-law and that one of the residents had caught on fire.

When we arrived on the scene, we discovered a very obese, deceased elderly woman.

She was probably in her seventies. We weren't sure if it was an accident or if it was a result of arson.

I was asked to go to the autopsy with my training officer. So, in my first two weeks on the job, I find myself at the coroner's office, with a dead body.

The outside of the body was charred to black chunks of ash. The few patches of skin that remained were falling off the body. The smell was absolutely horrible. It was atrocious. That smell is forever burned into my senses. For many months afterwards, if somebody was having a barbecue or somebody mentioned having barbecue, I couldn't actually eat because I recalled this incident.

I'm standing next to my field training officer, observing the coroner cut open the body. He's pulling her organs out. I've never seen a dead body up to this point, much less, a charred body being cut open and a full autopsy being done.

Suddenly, the coroner stops for a moment.

He says, "I think there's something in her throat."

At first, he can't tell what it is, so he gets some instruments and goes deep inside her throat. And right in front of me, he pulls a rag out of this woman's throat.

It turns out it was actually a homicide. Her son-in-law knocked her out, stuffed this rag all the way down her throat, and then lit her on fire.

That was the day I was first exposed to this truth: There is true evil in this world. This kind of evil is not something that you see on TV. It's not something you see in a movie. It's real.

The memory of her body, charred to ash, with a rag stuffed deep into her throat, and the smell of evil, clung to me for many years. Even now, I can put myself right back there at the coroner's office in Martinez. It doesn't matter whether I put Vicks vapor rub under my nose – I cannot get rid of that smell. In fact, to this day, if I'm cooking and my hand goes over the heat, causing the hair on the top of my fingers to burn a little, it brings the entire memory right back.

It's like a burnt hair smell, but a thousand times worse than that.

As I was standing in the coroner's office, I wanted to leave. I didn't want to be in that room. But I had to be there. As a rookie, I wanted to show my peers that this didn't bother me. I needed them to trust me and accept me as part of the team.

To witness a charred body cut open and all its organs spilling out - nobody should have to see that.

But I realized quickly that this is part of my job. I'm expected to deal with this and just move on. I remember my FTO (field training officer) joking about it. And I joked back with him. I learned quickly that this is how we handle these types of incidents.

Making jokes is a common coping mechanism for all first responders. Some people call it "gallows humor." It's a release – a dodge – a way of looking "strong" by making light of the awful things we see. It's a safeguard, and an internal defense mechanism.

No one – especially a rookie who is in training - would ever say, "Hey, you know, I don't appreciate the fact that you guys are laughing at this. This is actually really sick."

I was with the same field training officer when the second of these two calls came in. This one was a suicide attempt.

Since these first two calls, I've been to other homicides and tons of suicides – some where the gun was literally still smoking. But these two calls will always stick out in my mind. They were my first and they imprinted on me forever.

When the second call came in, we happened to be near the scene, so we got there first, before the firefighters or paramedics.

We ran up to the apartment and the door was opened by an older lady. She was the mother of the young lady who had attempted suicide. She was completely frantic, saying "Help! You've got to help my daughter!"

I entered the apartment. Her daughter was a very attractive woman who appeared to be in her early twenties. She had slit her neck with a knife. The cut was several inches long and so deep that I could see the fat in her neck. It looked like her head was going to fall off.

And she was totally calm. She had a deep gash on her neck, but she wasn't screaming. She didn't even act like she was in pain. She started talking about a Ouija board and the devil. She told me calmly that she was possessed by Satan. Meanwhile, blood was steadily flowing – not spurting - out of the 3-inch gash on her neck. I don't know how she didn't hit her carotid.

My FTO told me, "Look, you need to just keep talking to her, keep her engaged, keep her calm so she doesn't lose more blood before the paramedics get here."

So, I had to talk to this young lady and pretend like nothing was wrong even though it looked like her head was going to fall off.

Meanwhile, she continued to calmly tell us that she was possessed by Satan.

As soon as the medics got there, I felt a huge weight and burden lift off my shoulders. But until they showed up, it was just her and me, in that moment that will be forever frozen in my mind. At the time, I told myself, "I have to do this. I have to be strong. I'm being evaluated."

Like the other call, this was a defining event, in the sense that my view of the world changed in response to it. That day, once again, I saw the face of pure evil, not the young lady herself, but the thing that had overtaken her mind and body.

There is no training you can get – at any police academy – to prepare you for pretending that everything is just fine while someone sits there with a potentially lethal wound, calmly repeating that the devil made them do it.

Like the other time, my FTO and I joked about it – telling each other that she can get that thing patched up, but if she ever goes out, she'll need to wear a scarf around her neck. Humor was our only defense at the time – the only way to brush it off and move on.

Later in my career, I became a field training officer. And I did the same thing my FTO did on these two calls – I set the example that you can't show it when things bother you. I created the same feeling in those I trained – that strength is not showing your natural human reaction to horrifying things.

Back then, I wasn't looking at the officers I trained to see if these kinds of calls bothered them because I wanted to help them. At that time, I believed that showing emotions or expressing feelings meant that you were not a good fit for the job.

In this way, the culture gets formed and set. I learned it from those who came before me, and then taught it to those who came after me.

Now I see that changing the culture will require us to set a different culture from the earliest phases of police training. In a police department for instance, it starts in the academy and then with the examples set by field training officers.

The key to breaking the stigma is to normalize natural human responses by talking about them. When these kinds of calls happen, we need to take the time to talk about how this impacts us. This doesn't have to be a long ordeal, but we need to do this.

We typically debrief calls after the paramedics have taken control of the scene and we've done our paperwork. However, when we "debrief" these kinds of calls, we usually just talk about them in a factual, logistical way. We review what happened and discuss how we are going to document it.

But we never talk about the personal impact of these kinds of calls.

To change the culture, we need to do it from day one - in the training program, and everyone needs to be on board. For example, in a field training program, you may have four or five training officers. If even one of them sends the message that they're not affected by anything, it won't work. They all need to send the same message - these kinds of traumas have an impact on us.

Speaking for myself, as a new officer, even after being exposed to a few traumatic events during my previous years in the military, I had never experienced whatever this was - mental illness or spiritual warfare. It's a shock to realize that somebody could do this to themselves. The young lady who attempted to take her life had been well-groomed and looked completely normal. If you would've seen her on the street, you would have simply noticed her as an attractive woman. Other than evidence of the injury to her neck, there would be no indicators of the thoughts or voices in her head.

This event reminded me that outward appearances can be deceiving. And it forced me to confront the reality that death and pure evil are both out there, lying in wait. For someone in a first responder role, this translates into an awareness that every contact, every call we get, might be an encounter with this form of pure evil.

During training, they tell us that every call is potentially life ending. They tell us that domestic violence calls are the worst. But these kinds of calls wake you up and remind you of the reality of what you're doing.

I've watched movies. I've seen things like this before in them – actors speaking in that totally calm way about how the devil made them do something awful. But that's not real. When it's in your face and you're smelling it and you're seeing it in real time, it's very different. When you want to throw up, but have to pretend that it doesn't bother you, it is different than watching a movie.

The fact is that I still remember these things today. Here we are, talking about these two calls almost 17 years later. I've never talked about these events in my therapy sessions in the past. But guess what? These events really bothered me.

Doc Springer's Reflections

In my observation, one of the most overlooked sacrifices that is part of any warrior's life is the need to navigate two worlds. In conventional combat operations, anyone who deploys to a war zone finds themselves faced with an alternate reality – a world apart from the one at home. A world with different rules, and completely different experiences. Regardless of the training one receives, there is almost always a "trial by fire" element of the warrior's path. There is often the creation of a "split self" as well. Even those who do not sustain a "trauma exposure" often have difficulty during military transition, because two totally different worlds cannot be seamlessly knit into a common fabric. The two identities and two worlds must be held in tension, without losing one's fundamental "integrity," in the sense of integration of these experiences.

Like our military service members, our first responders also inhabit two worlds – the world known to most civilians and the world they face that few are privy to. In fact, the challenge of navigating two worlds is often *more difficult* for our first responders than for many of our military service members. They are exposed to an ongoing level of weekly trauma that can exceed the level of trauma sustained in a military deployment.

Our first responders regularly see the worst in humanity – the depths of depravity and the darkest evils in the world – and then they're asked to take off the uniform and be a loving spouse or a nurturing parent to their children. For our first responders, the two worlds they inhabit co-exist, and the psychological elasticity required to travel between these two worlds – what some might think of as "resilience" – is hard to put into words.

In the context of facing the kinds of evils Michael is describing, gallows humor is widely used as a coping strategy. People outside the world of a first responder might be tempted to judge the character of people who use gallows humor ("how could they make light of something so sick?") This impulse to judge shows how little many of us understand about the kinds of situations our first responders face on a continual basis. For many of them, their work involves a level of trauma that most of us can only imagine. And as Michael shares, understanding this reality in theory – or through seeing things like this in a movie – is entirely different from facing off against evil in real time.

As a psychologist who has held trust with our military and first responder community, it's important to me to make this point: there is nothing wrong with gallows humor. Many of the best people I know, with the biggest hearts, people who would lay down their lives for someone they've never met, will use gallows humor to cope with the traumatic impact of their work. They are good people. Gallows humor is a safe way for first responders to connect with each other.

However, gallows humor is not sufficient for managing unspeakable traumas. Using gallows humor as the only way of coping is like going into an active war zone armed with a .22 caliber pea shooter. To navigate two worlds without losing one's core integrity, it becomes critical to engage in deeper human connection. It becomes critical to speak truth in safe places with trustworthy people. And it becomes critical for us to create a culture of safety that allows for this to happen.

If safety cannot be created within the formal ranks, then it is vital that first responders have a safe outlet where they can give voice to unspeakable traumas. They must have a way to acknowledge the human impact of trauma – whether through a peer support program, or through a safe and trusted Doc. This connection becomes critical in the context of unimaginable traumas.

Connection is the armor that allows us to stare into the face of the Gorgon of evil. Connection is what allows humans to do superhuman feats. Connection sustains us during the valleys in our lives. When we connect, we survive.

3

NEAR DEATH EXPERIENCE

"White police officer draws his weapon on an African American kid." We often fill in the blanks on a headline like this, based on our own experiences and perceptions. Let's go back in time now, before the night of the fatal shooting, to Michael's memory of the first time he almost had to use lethal force on a suspect. Let's listen for the truth because the truth is often much more complicated than the headline.

* * *

The first time I almost shot someone, I looked nothing like a cop. I was working undercover on a drug task force at the time.

I had pierced ears, a shaved head, and a long goatee. I was wearing Air Jordans and baggy jeans, with a Skin Industries t-shirt. Picture a guy cast in a detective series as a "low-life, white drug dealer" and that's what I looked like (if you don't believe me, take a look at the picture we posted on our book page on Doc Springer's website: www.docshaunaspringer.com).

The fact that I didn't look like a cop, but a hardened street criminal, almost certainly played a key role in what developed.

There was a residential burglary that happened in the wealthy part of the city. Somebody broke into a house in the middle of the day, in the middle of a work week. Among other things, the burglar took a fully loaded, laser-sighted revolver from the house.

One of my good friends, an in-house Walnut Creek detective, was the primary person working this case. He hit me up to help him track down the burglar and we got a lead on who the suspect might be - a kid going to the high school near that house. We found out that this kid's mom worked at a local office complex.

Here are the events of that day, in real time.

We arrive at the office complex. It's a huge building, with multiple stories, the closest thing Walnut Creek has to a "city-sized building." Below the building is a four-story underground parking garage. Based on what we knew, we figured this kid may be involved, but we weren't a hundred percent sure.

So, as a first step, we decide to speak with his mother. I don't look like a cop, and my partner, who is in plain clothes, isn't in uniform either. He's an undercover detective and I look like a white gangster, an undercover role as part of my work with the regional drug task force. When we make contact with the mom, we immediately present our badges and ask her if she knows where her son is.

She says, "Look, I dropped him off at school this morning. I'm not sure where he is, but we have a routine where every day that I get off work, he makes his way back to this office building. I meet him at my car, parked in the garage downstairs."

He's not supposed to meet her at her car for many hours.

My partner and I go into the garage to scope out the car. We figure we can work out a game plan for hours later when he comes back to the car. We want to see where it's parked and take some pictures of the car. That way, we can get more detectives to provide backup for later in the day.

I've never been in this garage before. I'm not familiar with it. We don't know where the car is, but we know what it looks like, and we have the license plate number. So, we split up to look for the car.

Suddenly, I see the car. My partner is nowhere in sight. It's a white Volkswagen Passat. From a distance, it looks empty. I pull out my phone and I start taking pictures of the car and the license plate to help us develop our late afternoon approach. Suddenly, a head pops up in the back seat, startling me. My gun is concealed in my waistband, with a baggy shirt over it.

I yell for my partner, who is nowhere to be seen. The back door of the vehicle starts to fling open. I realize that I don't look like a cop. So, I immediately lift up my shirt. I don't know if he sees it, but I have my gun and my badge right there.

I said, "Hey, look, I'm a police officer. Everything's okay."

I'm trying to downplay why I'm contacting him because I don't even know if this kid is involved in the burglary. He is only a suspect at this time.

Apparently, while I was taking pictures, he was laying down on the back seat. As I'm trying to talk to him and stall him, hoping my partner will show up, he's able to get the door open. He starts running. I immediately start chasing after him.

Again, it's important to remember that I looked like a radical, militant white gangster - and he's an African American kid.

As I'm chasing him, he starts reaching down in his pants. If he is the burglar, then he's got a stolen laser-sighted revolver in his possession. He's a potential threat to anyone in that garage with this kind of weapon.

So I pull out my gun and I start screaming. "STOP! If you don't fucking stop, I'm going to fucking shoot you!" It all happens in a millisecond.

My finger is actually on the trigger as he's reaching down his pants. He starts turning towards me as he's running.

Thank God. I don't know why, but he immediately puts his hands out and stops running.

I yell at him to get on the ground.

When I search him, I find that he has the fully loaded revolver in his waistband.

And as soon as I secure the weapon, my partner comes running up. We handcuff him.

As soon as he is secured, I ask my partner, "Do you have him?" I have to step away. I can feel myself about to break down. My heart is racing. I've pulled my gun out before this, but this was the closest I've ever come to taking someone's life. And the fact is that he is just a young kid – maybe 15 or 16.

Later, when I interview him, I see that he's a nice kid. He's just a high school kid who made some really dumb decisions. It shocks me to the core.

If I had shot him, I would have been a hundred percent justified. He was reaching for a fully loaded gun. But the fact that I almost took his life and I'm sitting there talking to him, and he was respectful and apologetic, that hit me really hard. I said to him, "Man, I almost killed you."

When things calmed down, I fully internalized that I had almost killed this kid. I went into my supervisor's office, and I just lost it. I slumped to the ground, with my back against the wall, my whole body shaking.

But the same inner dialogue I always have after things go sideways takes over – "shake this sh-t off. You can't let this affect you. You can't show emotion." As police officers, we say to ourselves, "nothing's going to penetrate me. I'm just going to brush this off and move on to the next call. The next event."

I haven't spoken to anybody about this incident, until now. It really bothered me that I almost killed this kid. He wasn't a criminal or a bad person. He eventually confessed and ultimately was arrested and charged with residential burglary and possession of a stolen firearm.

But, at the end of the day, he was just a kid who did a bad thing. This wasn't somebody with a long rap sheet that was killing people, or raping people. He wasn't a gang member. He made a bad decision, but he was a good human being. This comes into play later when I actually had to take a life on December 27, 2012. In that situation, it was the same thing. This wasn't some cold-hearted career criminal. For all intents and purposes, he was also a good person.

I honestly think if I would have taken this kid's life, that would have been the end of my career right there. I truly do. And for the rest of my life, I would have had to live with the fact that I had killed a high school kid, with his whole life ahead of him, who really was a good person.

What I also learned that day was how quickly life can be taken - my own life or anybody else's life for that matter. It showed me how anybody can be killed like this, at any time, and it can happen very quickly.

Police officers are taught to project this image that we're invincible, like Superman or Superwoman. Most people don't realize that on the inside, we have the same feelings, emotions, and problems as everyone else.

I think that the public always sees us as stoic – somehow not fully human in the way that things impact us. But we are not invincible - these things absolutely affect us, often in permanent ways.

Doc Springer's Reflections

Like Michael, our warriors and first responders are often deeply protective by nature. They sacrifice, and they suffer, in order to protect those who can't protect themselves. Remember that during his time in the Air Force, Michael didn't complain after getting his ribs cracked during his Raven training exercises. He didn't pity himself, but instead said, "Ravens are the last line of defense. They can't fail in their mission to protect the people on the planes they protect."

After he transitioned from the military, becoming a police officer was a natural outlet for Michael's highly developed protective instincts. Simply put, it is a calling.

Those in law enforcement roles see the things most of us don't. They see how ugly and evil some people are. Some of us have a fantasy that everyone has some good in them. Turning a bad person good is a common trope in American movies. Think about all the movies we've seen that show an evil person transform into a loving person because someone else appealed to their better angels.

In reality, some people don't have better angels. To be influenced by others requires trust and connection. Some people have lost trust in others and have no instinct to connect or protect others. The fact is that there are some really bad people in the world – what psychologists would call sociopaths. I've seen them in my office. They are the people with dead eyes who live only to take from others.

Every person is just an object to them. They are devoid of empathy. They lack the capacity to connect with others. They won't change because someone else feels pain or wants them to change. In fact, they enjoy inflicting pain and feel entitled to take what they want, even when it destroys people's lives. They have no respect for law or rules, or basic decency. They defected from civil society a long time ago. They kill to get what they want, and sometimes, they kill for sport. These cold-hearted criminals actively target our police officers.

We seem to expect people in certain professions to have "psychological x-ray vision." Psychologists are asked questions like:

- "Is this convicted murderer really rehabilitated or will he kill again?

- Since both parents are accusing each other of child abuse, is one of them safe to be the caregiver for this child?

- Why did this person kill a roomful of innocent people for apparently no reason?

- If we release this person from the hospital, will she attempt to end her life?"

In the same way, we expect police officers to have "psychological x-ray vision" in determining people's intent.

How does one tell the difference between an armed sociopath who kills without remorse and someone who is not a bad person, but who is making some terrible choices?

It's very hard under normal circumstances to read intent based on a short interaction. It's even more difficult when one person is in a state of primal threat. And when both parties feel primally threatened, as in this situation, it's often impossible.

Fear cuts off our ability to see each other. When Michael first encountered this suspect, he realized that he did not look like a police officer. To this kid, he would have looked like a white drug dealer.

Because of this, Michael raised his shirt to show his badge. Did this high school kid see the badge? Probably not. Most likely, his focus was on the gun just next to the badge. When we are primally threatened, we focus like a laser on the potential threat to our life.

When he started to run, did this kid think about how the fully loaded revolver on his body would be a source of threat to everyone in that parking garage – the people that Michael has a duty to protect? Probably not. He was just running for his life, fueled by adrenaline and fear.

When Michael yelled, "STOP! If you don't f-cking stop, I'm going to f-cking shoot you!" did this kid hear the sub-text of Michael's communication? (His silent, but urgent plea, of "Please don't make me shoot you!!!) Perhaps not. On the other hand, perhaps it did break through since he suddenly stopped and surrendered his weapon to Michael.

Primal fear can make someone look like a threat – this can work both ways when two people are in a state of fear. And when someone like Michael – who is a Protector by nature, has to fire on, and potentially kill someone who isn't a bad person – it is one of the worst traumas a Protector can face.

4

STING

In the last chapter, Michael appeared in an undercover role. Let's go deeper now to uncover one of his greatest personal betrayals – which happened during his time with an anti-drug task force.

***

In 2009, I got the opportunity of a lifetime. The dream assignment I had always wanted since day 1 on patrol unexpectedly opened up – the chance to be part of the California Department of Justice Drug Task Force. I immediately jumped on it.

My mentor was Norm Wielsch, an experienced California Department of Justice Agent, named Commander of the Central Contra Costa County Narcotic Enforcement Team (CCCNET). Norm was one of the most accessible mentors I'd ever had. His door was always open. He talked about his family often. He would tell us how he would take his father on outings to casinos and other places his dad liked on the weekends. I came to Norm with all my questions about the craft of working undercover. He advised me on the right strategic decisions to make in the field.

Getting the job involved a competitive process that included an application, a ride-along, and an oral board. This long-term detail was for undercover work, which is how I ended up growing out my goatee and doing my best to imitate a drug-dealing scumbag.

Undercover work is very different from standard policing in a few important ways. First, we're undercover every single day. We don't wear a uniform. We grow our hair out, sometimes grow facial hair, drive cars that don't look like cop cars, and try to blend in. If you're working narcotics, you need to look like someone who belongs in the drug trade.

The only time you are identifiable as a cop is when you are part of an active operation, on a search warrant or a parole or probation search. In these cases, you have a long-sleeved t-shirt that says "police" on the arms, and a tactical vest that says "police" on the front and back. Of course, you also have your official belt and gun too.

Also, you are expected to manage your own time and be totally independent when working cases. As opposed to being tied to dispatch and waiting to be called into action that way, you are operating as an independent agent.

Going into a location to do a search for drugs is an adrenaline junkie's dream. Once you have the warrant, you have to knock on the door and identify yourselves as police first. You have to give them reasonable time to respond but you don't want to give them too much time. When they hear "Police!" at the door, one of two things could be happening. They could be arming themselves with guns, or they could be destroying evidence such as flushing drugs down the toilet.

Drug raids are the most dangerous thing we do. As a narcotics task force team, we're doing this more than a conventional SWAT team. The SWAT team may do one or two of these a month. We were doing this an average of 5 times a week. There were plenty of days where we did two operations in one day.

Back when I was undercover, drugs that are now legal were highly illegal. A minuscule speck of methamphetamine or cocaine would have been a felony. Possessing more than a tiny amount of marijuana or hash oil back then was a felony.

As a new guy or gal coming in, you don't really know anything about undercover operations. It's a steep learning curve, but at the same time, you feel an overwhelming pressure to be a superstar and you want to start making cases right away.

I'll never forget my first live operation…

***

I'm a brand-new narcotics agent and I've got a potential informant. I go through all the things we're supposed to do, and I decide that I'm going to give this person a chance. My informant reports on the location of an active drug house.

We're in a sketchy area. We set up an operation to send this person into the location to do a controlled buy of drugs. (For those who aren't aware, a "controlled buy" is one where we give them marked bills and maintain total control of the entrances and exits of the house. Sometimes, but not always, we have them wear a wire. When they come out of the house with the drugs, they turn them over to us, and that gives us the ability to execute a search warrant).

I'm really nervous because this is my first operation. I brief the team – to make sure everybody knows their job. We do a thorough search of the informant to make sure he has no drugs on him (because sometimes informants try to set people up to get out of jail time).

I watch the informant go into the residence. He purchases the drugs. We pick him up just afterwards and he hands me the drugs. Then we go to the judge. He signs a search warrant that gives us a set window of time to go in and do a search.

I plan the day that I want. The goal, during the raid, is to find evidence of drug sales. It's like gambling because drug dealers are constantly off-loading and uploading dope and cash. You never know. You may hit them, and find that they have all cash, but no dope, or all dope, but no cash, or, if you're lucky, you may get both. You want to get both.

I wasn't expecting much when we hit this house - maybe a little bit of drugs.

The rush of just going through that door is unforgettable. We go in with raid gear on, doors flying open, with our guns out. We're yelling at everybody, "Get down on the ground!" We're rushing through the residence to make sure nobody's hiding. Once we get everybody cuffed up, we go "code 4" which means that the setting is secure, and we can move on to the search.

The search is the fun part. Our whole goal is to find everything. Dealers are ingenious when it comes to hiding their supply. We've found things in walls, outlets, fake canisters and ceilings. I mean, you name it, and my team and I found a stash of drugs hidden there.

We hit the jackpot with this house. We ended up getting a huge quantity of methylenedioxymethamphetamine (MDMA, ecstasy, or "molly" as it's known on the street). He also had several pounds of marijuana, which was illegal at the time. And he had hundreds and hundreds of doses of Lysergic acid diethylamide (LSD), and a large quantity of mushrooms, along with about $25,000 in cash and evidence of sales all over the place.

So here I was, I was expecting maybe one kind of drug. And I ended up getting molly, marijuana, LSD and psilocybin. It was a righteous arrest. We had hit it out of the park. I could tell that my fellow agents were thinking, "Holy shit, who is this new guy?"

I felt totally pumped and so proud. I'll always remember the smile on Norm's face. It was like pleasing a parent. He was my mentor on the drug task force, the person I looked up to the most, and he was so proud of me.

We get back to our covert office which looks nothing like a police station, with everything we seized, loads of drugs. We go inside and I lay out all my evidence on the conference table. There's 25,000 dollars of cash spread out along with several bags of drugs. And Norm says, "You gotta take a picture with that."

At first, I resisted a little, but he said, "Look Michael, trust me. In this line of work, you're going to want to look back on days like this."

So, I put on latex gloves because this is evidence, and we don't want to touch the evidence. And I sit down at the end of this long wooden conference table with the entire stash laid out in front of me. In both hands, I'm holding up the two bags of Molly. I'm not smiling because that wouldn't be cool. I'm trying to look as hard as I can, like some dirt bag drug dealer holding these drugs, but inside, I was glowing. (You can take a look at the picture, since it's also included on Doc Springer's website page about our book – www.docshaunaspringer.com).

If you could have seen my thoughts, you'd know that I was thinking

"Man, this is exactly what I want. This is exactly why I'm here. This is what I was meant to do." When you walk into a drug house, good and evil are very clear. And nothing feels better than shutting down this kind of evil.

I'll never forget that day - that was a phenomenal day for me, a phenomenal memory. That was the day I fully became a part of the team, one of the guys who belonged on the task force.

During my time at CCCNET, as a California narcotics task force officer in Contra Costa County, I helped direct my team to many stings just like this. Together, we lifted a huge volume of drugs off the street, where they would have done damage to our communities.

While I was part of CCCNET, a former SWAT police officer turned private investigator named Chris Butler became the subject of a swirl of media attention. He had successfully pitched the idea of a reality show that was to air on Lifetime Television. Butler set himself up as a kind of "Charlie" as part of a "Charlie's Angels" arrangement with a circle of attractive young mothers. Butler made the point that the mothers with kids made ideal private investigators. Who would suspect a minivan-driving mother to be doing anything other than shuttling her children back and forth from their activities?

Butler had surrounded himself with a circle of women eager and ready to do various things at his request. During a profile of this arrangement on 48 Hours Mystery, on an episode entitled "Soccer Moms Confidential" several women voiced their enthusiasm for being "undercover operators." It was an exciting proposition for them. When Lifetime TV signed on to film them, they no doubt had fantasies of becoming household names just like the women in various "Housewives of..." reality shows.

It's not clear from the 48 hours profile whether all the women were aware and complicit in staging the reality show. But when Peter Crooks, the Senior Editor of Diablo magazine joined them at their invitation for a ride-along, it became clear to him that it was all fake – all of it scripted and acted by decoys. Crooks also discovered that Butler had staged cases for national media outlets, including People magazine and the Dr. Phil show.

In a piece entitled "The Inside Story of Contra Costa's dirtiest Drug Bust," published by Diablo Magazine on March 21, 2011, Crooks describes how the story developed into a "twisted tale involving illegal narcotics sales, product placement firearms, dirty DUI stings, and the terrifying possibility of military-grade explosives posing a threat to the community."

In the article, Crooks describes Butler as "incredibly corrupt and megalomaniacal" and says that "It seems as if he was trying to be the star of Magnum, P.I. and Scarface at the same time."

It turns out that Butler was not working alone. He had a partner.

I didn't know it at the time, but I was wire tapped for a California DOJ police-corruption probe that resulted in the prosecution of officers from Danville and San Ramon. The wiretap proved my innocence and identified the hidden ringleader, Norm Wielsch, the Commander of the Narcotics Task Force.

Norm was sentenced to 14 years in federal prison on charges of stealing drugs out of police evidence lockers, selling crystal methamphetamine, anabolic steroids, and marijuana, running prostitution rings, robbing prostitutes, and making false arrests.

Wielsch's attorney attempted to make the argument that depression and PTSD, as well as the influence of Chris Butler were the reasons for years of calculated criminal behavior. According to an article in the East Bay Times, at one point, Wielsch claimed that he wanted to stop robbing prostitutes, but Butler blackmailed him into continuing by claiming that he had video of (married) Wielsch having sex with one. The judge didn't buy it.

As it turns out, since Norm knew the state of play with all active operations, he was able to direct stings to his competitors and warn people in his network when a sting was planned in one of his areas of operation. In this way, he was able to evade discovery for quite a long time. And Wielsch and his cronies took their competitor's stash and resold it to benefit themselves. It sickened me to think of the risks we took to get dangerous drugs off the street, only to have them resold by a bunch of dirty cops. To say that I felt used is only the beginning.

As a result of Wielsch's corruption, the task force was permanently disbanded. It was a crushing blow to me, personally and professionally. Professionally, through no fault of my own, I lost my dream of being an undercover agent working major drug cases. My whole career up to that point had been focused on drug arrests, turning informants, finding weapons, and ultimately taking drugs off the street. Because of these dirty cops, including my own mentor, my dream got shattered forever. My plan was to be undercover as long as I could - hopefully four to five years - but the task force got disbanded after just two years. So, it changed my path and made me reconsider my goals and my purpose.

When something like this happens, even if you are innocent, people look at you differently - not only people in my agency, but others on the joint task force, and people in the court system including judges. CCCNET worked with agents assigned from all different agencies within Contra Costa County. Previously, I was the drug expert. I would go to court not just for my own cases, but for other officers' cases too. I was the go-to expert.

There was a period during the investigation where I wasn't allowed to talk to other people, and I began to feel like a suspect. I was actually interrogated as part of the internal affairs investigation. For years, I had given my all to this community, to this agency, only to be treated like a suspect. I was made to feel like I'd done something wrong when in fact I hadn't. When all the facts came to light, I was cleared of all suspicion – but the process left a stain on my reputation regardless.

When this broke, I went from being at the top of my game, very well-respected and absolutely trusted, to working under a continual shadow of doubt. It felt like a dark cloud covered everything I did, regardless of my proven innocence. It felt like people were looking at me and thinking, "Hey, is this guy involved? Is he part of this? How did he not know? How could he not have seen the signs?"

Looking back now, I can see some of the signs. But at the time, I couldn't see them. None of us did. To all of us, it was inconceivable to be betrayed like this.

For me, this event led to a sudden loss of trust and confidence in someone who I considered not only a friend and coworker, but a leader, and a mentor. Norm was someone that I looked up to. He was considered a narcotics interdiction expert and was widely respected by officers across the county. I was in shock - absolute shock. I couldn't believe it. At first, I thought somebody was playing a joke on me. When I found out that it was true, my trust just totally shattered.

I think this experience caused me to not trust people as much as I used to. I was painfully reminded that outward appearances and looks can be very deceiving. I learned to not trust, but to always be on guard and quickly size people up. As police officers, we're expected to analyze people in seconds. We get pretty good at it, but we're not always right. This experience reminded me to not get complacent. After this happened, I told myself that I couldn't assume that any environment or person was safe. It's better to always be on guard.

It wasn't until many years later that I started to trust (a few people) deeply again.

Doc Springer's Reflections

The late Dr. Charles Ducey was one of my favorite professors during my time at Harvard. He wasn't the sort of professor who merely recounted the doings of "great people" – he was a *thinker.*

During one of our conversations, Dr. Ducey made a comment that I'll never forget. We were talking about how children with continually traumatic childhoods can sometimes emerge as healthy adults who break the cycle of abuse. This is what he said: "If a kid has just *one adult* who is o*n their side,* who really *sees* them and *invests in them,* they can *survive* a traumatic childhood. It doesn't have to be a biological parent. In many cases, it's a grandparent, an aunt or uncle, or someone who is not even related, like a teacher or high school athletic coach. As long as they have one person like this, they can make it."

His observation captures what I've seen in my work with those who have suffered layers of complex trauma. In the LEO (law enforcement officer) community, trust is a very fragile and precious thing. Even among warm-hearted, service-driven individuals who would lay their life down in the line of duty, trust in others is not a default position. Distrust is the default position. For first responders and those in the military community, trust must be earned.

When trust is extended, it comes after the other person sees evidence that someone is trustworthy. The circle of deep trust is kept very small among those in these communities. Trusting the wrong person can cost you your life, or the lives of those around you.

Because so few are able to earn the trust, those who do, become "trust bearers." Don't google that – I just made it up, to explain this concept. Imagine two people, one of whom has many deep and trusting relationships. Now, imagine someone who has just a couple people that they trust very deeply. In this analogy, the first person is like someone who has well diversified investments in a financial profile, while the other is like someone who has all their money invested in just a couple stocks. In the former scenario, with a diversified portfolio, the failure of one stock does not bring financial ruin. Other investments buffer against the impact of this. In the case of someone who has all their money invested in just a couple companies, if one fails, it's a disaster. Our network of trust can work the same way.

For someone in Michael's position, as a new member of the narcotics task force, Norm was a deeply trusted mentor. Like many other members of the LEO community, he was a "trust bearer" in the sense that the trust Michael placed in him was rare, and symbolically important. This kind of trust is a buffer against the traumatic impact of the job. When people within a small circle of belonging – such as the tight knit group within the CCCNET task force hold trust with each other, they can endure the fear, trauma, and loss that is part of their work.

When this trust is broken by a "trust bearer," the psychological impact is hard to calculate. A violation of this kind of trust is more than a deeply felt, personal betrayal. It's a defining moment that often leads to a long struggle to trust anyone, ever again.

While Michael's stories are unique to him, the personal impact of this kind of within-group betrayal is commonly felt among members of the LEO community. The loss of trust with one of the few people one has been able to trust is an attachment wound of the highest order. And it does long-term psychological damage.

5

SOLITARY CONFINEMENT

As soon as the fatal shooting happened, Michael went into solitary confinement, in his mind. This place of extreme isolation and private suffering would become his new normal for many years to come.

This chapter takes us to the time just after the shooting.

✳✳✳

(December 27, 2012)

Just after the shooting, I called my wife to say, "Something just

87

happened. I'm fine. But I'll be home much later than usual." That was all I was allowed to say. I called her because I didn't want her to worry about me.

Privately, I felt like I was suddenly living in a bad nightmare. But I couldn't communicate any of this at the time.

At the time, I was in disbelief and shock. How could this have happened? Not in the city where I work. This never happens. There hadn't been an officer-involved shooting in Walnut Creek for at least 12 years.

Any time there is an officer-involved shooting, the involved officers are automatically put on administrative leave. In addition, there are two simultaneous investigations that happen as a result – one led by Internal Affairs (IA) within the police department, and an external investigation that is conducted through the District Attorney's office (the DA).

For those outside the LEO community, the IA investigation is like a root cause analysis within a health care or corporate setting. The big question for the IA investigation is whether any of the involved officers violated any policies or procedures. For example, was the use of force called for? Was force used according to correct practice and policy? In an IA investigation, officers are legally required to answer all questions they are asked. They have no right to "plead the fifth." Giving up this right is standard practice in the police community.

An IA investigation can get you fired while a District Attorney (DA) investigation – which happens outside the police department - can get you put in prison.

For this reason, there were two separate processes where I had to provide evidence – including photographs taken of me, and closeups of my hands, for the purpose of these different investigations.

As I shared previously, evidence was collected as soon as I returned to the department. There was a second round of evidence collection hours later, after I was taken to the local Marriott hotel, along with the other officers from the scene. We were separated throughout this process – intentionally sequestered in different rooms so that we could not talk and compare stories.

I remember that it felt weird at the time- like I was being snuck into the hotel. A reserve officer named Allen escorted me. Allen and I were close, and I desperately wanted to talk to him about what I was thinking and feeling. But I was reminded to not say a word about the shooting to anyone, other than the legally appointed investigators.

This was drilled into us. We could lose our jobs if we talked to anyone else. To add to the weirdness I was feeling, here I was with one of my closest friends, someone I trust completely, and I couldn't talk about the fact that I almost got killed a few hours ago. I wasn't physically alone because my friend was there, but I felt completely alone because I couldn't discuss anything that had happened.

When I got to my room, my head was spinning from sheer exhaustion. I had broken down sobbing two times, and my guts felt sore, the way you do when you've been vomiting for several hours.

My body needed sleep, but my soul needed to understand. So, instead of sleeping, I was constantly flipping back between KTVU, KRON, and KPIX - all the San Francisco Bay area news stations. The shooting was all over the news, but with no details at all.

Just after the shooting, there was an independent reporter, the kind of person who scans police calls and hopes to "make a scoop." But he was outside the residence, and his footage showed only the front door and the alleyway beside it.

No details were reported on any of the news channels. The Police

Department held all the details close to the chest. Nowadays, there is a standard process after incidents like this. The media gets invited to a briefing, where they are given a PowerPoint presentation, allowed to listen to the dispatch tapes, and to see the footage from body cameras worn by the involved officers.

There is a lot more transparency now, and the facts are shared with the public quickly, as in, "here's what the 911 caller said, here's what the officer saw…."

But back in 2012, it wasn't standard practice to put everything out there like that. They didn't use technology back then like we do now. There were no PowerPoint slides or reviews of body cam footage.

This was a problem. Here's why: When they didn't explain that we defended ourselves against someone who had actively assaulted us with a butcher knife, it raised questions about our character. We were totally undefended in the court of public opinion. In the weeks and months to come, rumor and speculation replaced facts. The fact that the suspect even had a butcher knife didn't come out at the initial press interviews with the police department. The lack of information from the department about the threat we faced, and our prohibition from talking about it, forced us into silence while no one else stepped up to speak the truth.

When you don't understand the context of a situation, you're likely to draw false conclusions. This was not a normal call. This was a call that came from a dispatcher who was in a state of panic, telling us that an armed assailant was attacking someone with a knife.

As I drove to the scene, the picture in my mind was one of entering a residence covered in blood. At the police department, we are provided with boxes of black latex gloves for the jobs we do.

They're like the blue ones that healthcare workers use, but they are black in color, because having bright blue hands could get you noticed and killed. When getting ready to go out for my shift, I would literally grab two handfuls of these latex gloves and stick them in the pockets of my uniform's cargo pants.

Not every officer is the same, but for me it was a habit, for two reasons. First, I wanted to protect myself from coming into contact with MRSA, HIV, hepatitis, and other bloodborne pathogens and bacteria. For the same reason I always carried sanitizing wipes or hand sanitizer, I put on gloves anytime I expected to have contact with people or body fluids.

Anytime I thought I would have to make personal contact with a person or collect evidence, I put on gloves to protect both myself, the person, and the crime scene.

The other reason I wore gloves was to protect crime scene evidence. You don't want your fingerprints to contaminate evidence.

And in this case, as I was driving to this call, I was envisioning blood everywhere. I already thought that someone had been fatally stabbed. And hearing the blood curdling screams when I arrived at the scene, I was prepared to walk into a blood bath. So, as I always did, I put on a pair of black latex gloves.

Since people who do not do police work lack this context, this became another example of how we got damaged in the court of public opinion. During the trial, the defense made up crazy theories – including suggesting that we wore gloves because we entered the residence with the intent to kill someone and hide the evidence. (How does that work? Four different police officers decide to kill a total stranger for no apparent reason, and bury the evidence of this evil deed?)

The defense pulled all kinds of stunts, making me put the gloves on in public during the trial proceedings, and as lawyers sometimes do, trying to create an entirely different story from what actually happened.

Although there were four police officers involved in this shooting (myself, another male, and two females), the male and I were the target of the trial proceedings. All four of us had been granted "qualified immunity" for the first round of shots fired. For those unfamiliar with the concept, qualified immunity grants legal immunity to law enforcement officials who act in good faith during rapidly evolving legal situations.

When the ballistics reports came in, it was determined that only me, and the other male officer, were involved in the second round of shots, and the rounds we had fired had killed the assailant. So, the legal focus was on the two of us, not the other officers, and the burden of defense was to show that lethal force had been justified.

In this kind of a pressure cooker situation, details matter. Lawyers look to exploit any differences in what people remember and what they later learn to be true.

For example, just after the night of the shooting, I was asked about why the front door of the residence had been damaged. I had no memory of why that would be the case, so I simply said, "I don't know."

A few days later, when I had gotten some sleep, I woke up one night at 3 a.m. in a cold sweat, with a vision of myself kicking at the front door, trying to get in. I called my lawyer first thing the next morning, my heart pounding the whole time. I was worried that since I didn't initially remember kicking at the door, I would be in serious trouble when it came out – and no one would take my word on anything I might say to defend myself.

Same thing with my memory of who was standing next to me, as we both simultaneously fired our weapons to neutralize the threat coming at us. I thought that it was the female police officer that first arrived at the scene. I had no idea that she had retreated and that another officer, one of our back-up responders, had been the one standing right next to me. I had no idea.

It was alarming to me that I had no recall of some things (like trying to kick in the door) and my memory of other things, including who was standing right next to me, were not accurate. I was so focused on the butcher knife that everything else was a blur.

Here's the critical thing to understand. In police work, our memories are the basis of our reports. We develop very keen memories of details as a result. Normally, I remember things in detail, and very accurately. I know this because other officers independently corroborate the same set of observations. It was a new thing for me to not have good recall of a situation.

I was terrified that what I couldn't remember might cause me to lose everything – to be labeled a cold-blooded killer, instead of a police officer working to protect everyone on the scene from an armed assailant. I had frequent nightmares about losing everything – going to prison for homicide and losing my family as a result – all because I couldn't remember every detail from the night of the shooting with the accuracy I was used to.

***

The day after the shooting, while we were sequestered in our rooms at the Marriott, we were each introduced to our attorneys – all of us assigned separate lawyers from the same law firm. Once we had met with our lawyers, we were accompanied by them as we did the DA interview in a conference room at the Marriott.

I had been up for 24 hours at that point. Beyond exhausted, and with no safe place to talk about what had just happened, I lost it during the interview and started bawling in front of both the investigators and my supervisor. It was so embarrassing, but I had no choice – it all just flooded out of me in that moment.

After completing the interviews at the Marriott Hotel, we were allowed to go home. I remember thinking, "thank God an officer from my department can drive me home." I lived about 35 minutes away and was in no condition to drive.

By the time I arrived home, I was totally numb. My wife had been waiting and watching for me to arrive. She opened the door with our daughter in her arms. I gave them both a quick hug that I didn't feel and told them I needed to sleep.

At the time, I was on the night shift, so I had put blackout curtains on all my windows. It made the room, during daytime, as pitch black as the middle of the night.

I walked into this dark cave that was my room and crashed for many hours, sleeping late into the night.

When I woke up, I made a decision that I'll always regret. I decided I would not tell my wife what had happened. I had almost died and, as a result, I was struggling with an overwhelming fear of dying. I was having panic attacks and nightmares. I didn't want my wife to have that fear.

It was almost a feeling that my fear might be contagious to her, and so I put myself in quarantine to protect her. I didn't want her to "catch" this feeling of fear. I didn't want her to suddenly realize, as I had, that I could die on any call I might go out on.

Between the prohibition to talk to anyone about the shooting, and my decision to shield my wife from this fear of death, I became totally isolated and suffered in silence for many years. During that time, the fear and the trauma ate me alive.

Isolating myself in this way was the worst thing I could have done. Now that I've been in therapy, and been able to talk about this trauma, and this fear, I see how talking to someone I trusted would have protected me and my loved ones from losing connection with each other.

My wife was patient for a long time, but ultimately, this change in me, our loss of connection, and the ways that I was self-destructing led to our divorce in the midst of the trial that was to claim the next few years of my life.

Doc Springer's Reflections

For this particular reflection, I have to step aside from being purely an objective observer, in order to back Michael up in some of his observations about how memories can be distorted because of a traumatic event.

Some of my understanding comes from objective research – for instance, as a psychologist, I'm well familiar with the work of researchers who have shown us just how inaccurate "eyewitness" testimonies can be. In fact, one of the leading researchers, a person who removed the scales from our eyes on this fact, is Dr. Gary Wells, who I knew during my time at Iowa State University. One of his graduate students, who became Dr. Elizabeth Olson, was even my roommate one year. In 2003, Dr. Wells and Dr. Olson wrote a paper to assert that mistaken eyewitness identification has been the single largest factor contributing to the wrongful conviction of innocent people.

But, as we all know, it's one thing to know something in theory, and another to experience it on a personal level. I know personally what it's like to lose chunks of memory because of a trauma. Specifically, a recent conversation with my sister revealed how holes in our memory can persist over decades.

During my undergrad years at Harvard, there were several local bars, frequented by college students, and locals alike. As an athletic young woman, I had a false sense of invulnerability. At the time, I had a regular weightlifting partner who was a guy, and I used to do night runs with some of the guys I was friends with from Harvard. I was president of the Harvard Cuong Nhu martial arts club. Cuong Nhu is a martial art that combines seven major "hard" and "soft" martial art styles: Japanese Karate, Aikido and Judo; Vietnamese Vovinam; Chinese Wing Chun and Tai Chi; and European Boxing. In fact, "Cuong Nhu" translates to "hard, soft" for this reason. In those days, I often roamed the streets of Cambridge at night, by myself, without fear.

So, it was normal for me to walk over and arrive alone at a local bar to meet up with a few of my friends. One night, I noticed that there was no line outside. It was bitterly cold. There was a large, thirty-something-year-old man standing outside, where the bouncer would usually be. I had been to this bar several times but had never encountered him. I walked up to him and assuming he was there to check IDs, I started digging in my purse for my wallet.

Before I knew it, he had me in a headlock and had started to drag me into a nearby alleyway. There was a whole bar full of people inside and this all played out literally just a few feet away from all of them. No one intervened. It's possible they didn't even see it (were the windows fogged up on this bitterly cold night? I can't remember).

Anyway, my sister asked me, "did you scream for help?"

Here's the thing - no, I didn't scream for help. Calling for help, yelling "HELP!" or "RAPE!" at the top of my lungs might seem the most "logical" thing to do, but I didn't say a word. I DO remember being hyper-focused on finding any part of his body that I could hurt, badly, so that he would release me from the headlock. I found an ear. With all my strength, I ripped down on that ear until it was hanging from his head by a thin piece of flesh. He let go.

My sister said, "So, what happened next? Did you go inside the bar and meet up with your friends? Did you report it?"

And the truth is that I didn't. The details of what happened after that are ones I've re-constructed in my mind, to put the puzzle pieces together.

That on this bitterly cold night, the real ID-checker was just inside the door. This man was posing as a bouncer just outside. Maybe he was in the bar, with a few drinks in him and had come outside for a smoke. And maybe when I mistook him as the bar's ID-checker and dropped my guard to dig around in my purse, he saw me as easy prey and took the opportunity to assault me.

What I recall is that after the assault, somehow, I went straight home, back to the safety of my dorm room, and I sat in my room, in the dark, until my heart stopped hammering in my chest. It felt like hours before my heart returned to a normal rhythm. As soon as this happened, though, this thought emerged with crystal clarity: "I cannot say a word about this to anyone. If I do, my attacker will know my identity and he could sue me for what I did to his ear. If I explain that it was done in self-defense, what happens if no one believes me? I can't risk it. It's better that I just keep this to myself."

How I got back to my dorm after the assault is lost to my memory

– my understanding is a patchwork reconstruction of what probably happened based on a few things. The dorm was well within distance for a quick run. After he let go of me, my assailant probably staggered off into the night holding his bleeding face, and I probably ran home as fast as I could. That's the pattern – I had done this before at a party in high school when I was in a potentially dangerous situation. I had no ride, but the party was just a few miles from my house. So, I scooped up my shoes and ran home. A natural thing to do since I ran cross-country at the time.

I also know with total clarity that during this assault outside the bar, I didn't say a word or make any sound of distress. As I said, I certainly didn't report the assault, not even to others who I love and trust, not until more than 20 years had passed. When I hear stories of people who have sustained a sexual trauma, I remind myself that I am frankly just lucky this didn't happen to me. It certainly could have.

Here's what I learned from this experience. When one feels primally threatened, the hyper-focus on the source of the threat, and associated gaps in memory are a real thing.

In reflecting on my own experience, I appreciate the deeply vulnerable place that Michael was in. For whatever reason, we seem to assume that our police officers are not fully human – that even when their lives are threatened, they should be able to exercise perfect recall, in the ways they have been trained to observe and report. Add to this the fact that trial attorneys are skilled at identifying any inconsistencies in a person's story, which can lead people to doubt the credibility of a witness. During our prep for this chapter, Michael told me that when he realized he was not able to recall things clearly from the night of the shooting, he became "paranoid about not remembering" other important things.

In the context of the legal battle that ensued, this is not paranoia. Michael was fighting the darkness, and in the end, the darkness claimed his marriage.

6

ACCUSED

Whenever there is an officer-involved shooting, there are multiple inquiries and proceedings that follow. In this chapter, Michael will walk us through the critical incident debriefing, the coroner's inquest, and the internal meeting that happened behind closed doors with his administration.

***

After a week at home, myself and the other officers involved in the shooting were brought into a critical incident debriefing.

A critical incident debriefing is always attended by a contracted therapist as well as the officers who are directly involved in the incident. So, in this case, the meeting was attended by me, four other officers, the dispatcher, and the therapist.

The therapist in this case was one that had worked for the department for some time. We all knew and liked her, and we all knew and liked each other. In theory, this would have been a perfect place to openly discuss how we were impacted by the fatal shooting. But this isn't what happened during the meeting. It usually isn't what happens in these circles.

I was the ranking officer in the group. I had already broken down in tears twice – once just after the fatal shooting, and once during the interviews in the Marriott Hotel conference room. I desperately wanted to get back to work and feel normal again. I didn't want anyone to doubt my ability to lead. I was still on probation as I had just been promoted to the role of sergeant. I didn't want to show any more vulnerability than I already had.

My mentality was "Let's get through this. Let's get this done."

In these scenarios, everyone has a need to put the pieces of the puzzle together. We had all lived through that night together but had not been able to speak to anyone about what had happened to us. During the debriefing, we were like sponges, craving any little piece of information from each other to form a clear picture of what happened that night. Putting this together is therapeutic in a sense. But it's not the same thing as taking the opportunity to talk about how this had impacted all of us, personally.

Now that I understand what it takes to heal from a trauma like this, I would have shared all of this with them, regardless of my rank. In fact, I would now use my rank to set a culture where others could share the same, without shame or judgment. But none of this happened that day. I did not have the understanding then about the importance of this kind of emotionally transparent communication.

It's also hard to be open when you are under investigation, which can feel like being under attack.

We had two active investigations underway, and I was instructed very firmly to not talk with anybody about the events of that night. In addition, the officers on the scene, including myself, got sued immediately by the family in a prolonged civil lawsuit that dragged on for almost four years. Four years…where I had to relive that night over and over, sitting through constant depositions with the father of the man I killed staring at me for eight hours a day.

***

The coroner's inquest, on August 5, 2013, was a particularly low point, another day that I'll never forget.

Anytime there is a death where officers are present, there's a coroner's inquest – whether it's an in-custody death, a fatal car accident from pursuit, or an officer-involved shooting. The point of the inquest is to determine the mode or manner of death, and whether it was accidental or not.

In our county, the coroner's inquest takes place in a courtroom. There's a judge and a full jury. It's open to the public. At the time of the coroner's inquest, my marriage was already starting to fall apart. My drinking was getting out of control.

I invited my wife to the inquest because I hadn't told her what had happened.

Over months of suffering in silence, I couldn't find the words to tell her what I'd been going through. I wanted her to be at the inquest so she could hear it for herself. My hope was that by having her there, I wouldn't have to explain it to her. She could just experience it and hopefully understand it. I hoped she might be able to understand me and what I had been going through. I held onto hope that it would help relieve the strain in our relationship for her to really understand it.

On the day of the inquest, there were several reporters, and in addition to my wife, there were about 20 different people from my agency. The family members of the deceased were also there – his grandparents, his parents, and his stepparents.

Not only them, but it turns out that the man I shot had an identical twin brother who looked just like him. He was there too, his eyes full of rage.

I was in the courtroom, waiting to testify, and all eyes were on me as I heard the dispatch tapes for the first time since the night of the shooting. Hearing the calls over the radio – the sheer panic in the dispatcher's voice – it immediately sucked me right back to that night.

I started sweating profusely. The hairs on the back of my neck stood up, my heart started pounding and I felt like I was going to pass out. It was worse than a "flashback." It was like being there on the night of the shooting, but with the awareness that it ended in the death of the man I shot.

And in that state of mind, I was asked to get up on the stand. The jury panel was sitting just a few feet away from me. I was asked to tell everyone assembled there what happened.

As I'm telling it, some among the jury were looking at me in a fearful or shocked way. I hadn't been able to process any of this with a single safe person until the day of the inquest. This was the first time I had to tell the whole story in graphic detail, and I did it in front of the eyes of a jury, a judge, my colleagues, my wife, the man's family, and his identical twin brother. It was too much.

I ended up losing it and breaking down, crying in this courtroom of literally 60 people. People I work with. People I don't know. I was crying like a baby.

I've never cried like this in my entire life. This isn't something I do. I'm a former Air Force officer. I'm a police sergeant. I don't cry – and if I do, I definitely don't do it in a courtroom. But like the two times before, on the night of the shooting and during the interviews at the Marriott, I became flooded with emotions I couldn't control.

I was so ashamed and so embarrassed that the judge said, "Thank you, sergeant. We have what we need. You're excused."

There was a quick recess and then the other officers testified. They did a good job and we got through it.

About two weeks later, one of my administrators called me into the office. At the time, I was thinking, 'This is good. We did well. We saved the lives of two people who were being attacked by a man with a butcher knife and we saved the lives of the officers that he turned on next. Other than the assailant, no one else got hurt. The coroner's inquest determined that our actions were warranted and appropriate to the situation.'

At the time, I thought I was getting called in to be praised for doing my duty in an honorable way. Before the shooting, I had been promoted to sergeant over other officers more senior than myself. And in the months after the shooting, I continued to perform well at work. I was fully operational – and totally back in the zone when on the job. When I was at work, I felt invincible, like a shining star in the department with an incredibly bright future ahead of me. Of course, no one knew that at home, I was cut off from my wife, drinking alcohol, and sleeping the days away.

Based on my performance at work, the story in my head was that I had advanced through the ranks quickly, and had performed well under pressure, protecting those around me when lives were in danger.

When I walked into the room, there were a couple of administrators in there. And I felt a shift inside me. This isn't good. Every instinct is telling me this is *not good*.

I love my agency and there are some great people there, but this was a pivotal moment in my decision-making process to not get help. What happened during that interaction caused me to spiral down the path of self-destruction that followed.

The first thing that happened is that they questioned the genuineness of my emotions during the coroner's inquest. They suggested that I was acting or putting on a show for the jury. Can you imagine me as a grown man in my forties – a veteran and Captain of the Air Force, a police sergeant, who hasn't gotten emotional his entire life, wanting to break down in public like that?

By questioning the authenticity of my grief and trauma, they called my fundamental integrity into question.

And then my leadership abilities got called into question. Not once did anyone ever check in on me, as in, "Hey, can we do something for you? Can we get you some help?"

What they did do is to extend my probationary status as a sergeant – indefinitely - which put my promotion in jeopardy. It was devastating. I was so embarrassed and worried that other people I worked with and led would find out. Here I thought I was a total rock star in the department, and now my very identity and future were being called into question.

When this happened, I made a mistake. I didn't speak up for myself because I was a military guy. If you outranked me, and especially if you're in command or an administrator, it was "Yes, sir. Yes, ma'am. No, sir. No, Ma'am" and that was it. There wasn't going to be any questioning. There wasn't going to be any backtalk. I was taught to nod my head, accept it, and press on with the mission.

And that's what I did. In fact, I made a conscious decision that day. I decided that I would never show emotion again. I was never going to show weakness. I was going to prove them wrong.

As I left that meeting, with my cheeks burning, I said to myself, "You know what? Fuck this! I'm going to prove you guys all wrong!"

To be blunt, I became an asshole. I became unapproachable. I didn't care. I wasn't sympathetic. I wasn't empathetic. I didn't want to hear what anyone had to say. If I was supervising someone and they had a problem, my response at the time was "that doesn't sound like a problem to me."

I was thinking to myself the whole time, "You have no idea what it means to have a problem."

And that's how much I lost sight. I lost sight of my purpose as a supervisor and as a leader. On multiple occasions, my administrators said to me, "People are coming to us, saying that you're unapproachable and hard to talk to."

I shut everyone out and was numb to their pain, and my own.

Not once did any of my administrators say, is everything okay with you? How's the marriage? How's your health? How are your relationships doing?

And to be honest, since I didn't trust them anymore, even if they had asked me, I wouldn't have told them a thing. I would have continued the sham and said, "Nope. Everything's good."

The truth? My marriage was over. I was going through a divorce. I was either drinking or sleeping the days away anytime I was not on duty. I was being sued by the assailant's family in federal civil court in San Francisco - one of the most anti-cop places in the country. I was in danger of losing everything and everyone that I loved.

Doc Springer's Reflections

Trauma can drastically change our personalities. Anyone who has met Michael in the past few years would find it hard to recognize him in the person described above – "unapproachable," "unsympathetic" and cold are not terms that describe who Michael is today – quite the opposite. In fact, one of the things that inspired me to partner with Michael for this project is that he is empathic to others who suffer, and vulnerable in sharing his own story. This is who Michael is now, after coming through the valley of his trauma.

Trauma can change our personalities in a single instant in some cases. Many of my patients have said things like "something snapped in me that day" or "that was the day I decided to be….". As in Michael's case, the change can be the result of a conscious decision. And often when it is, this is in reaction to the deepest, most personal kind of betrayal between humans. The kind of betrayal Michael describes here is the exact opposite of what promotes healing from trauma. It makes the cut so much deeper. With the kind of betrayal Michael is describing, others in his life trampled all over the sacred ground of his personal vulnerability.

It's the opposite of what a trusted Doc would do. A trusted Doc would have held space for Michael to say and feel whatever he needed to express without judgment, with understanding and compassion. A safe person would have witnessed all of it without altering their opinion of Michael. A safe person would have created a way for Michael to address his trauma with his dignity intact. A worthy healer is a warrior in their own way and would have offered a protective shield for him to heal as he fought the darkness.

In the courtroom on the day of the coroner's inquest, Michael didn't choose to be vulnerable – he had no choice. He broke down, as even the strongest among us would do, under the overwhelming stress of the moment. If you have ever struggled with Post-Traumatic Stress, imagine having a vivid flashback while on a witness stand in an open courtroom, breaking down in front of people you don't know, and people like your husband or wife, that you depend on for connection.

When his administrators questioned Michael's integrity, the weight of his trauma was layered with something different - moral injury. This made the deep cut of trauma ten times deeper and led to years of additional pain, as Michael became someone other than who he is in his core. This is not uncommon after trauma. I can't tell you how many of my patients have said things like, "I've *become an a—hole*. This isn't who I was before" in the wake of unaddressed trauma.

At other times, trauma comes repeatedly, like a thief in the night, stealing little pieces of our lives over time. As we lose little parts of ourselves, and change in incremental ways, this has an impact on our loved ones. We may not realize that we are changing, but those who love us absolutely feel the change. To see us suffering and to not understand the cause of our pain creates a high level of anxiety for those who love us. And this can stress our relationships to a breaking point.

Part of the reason for this is that trauma causes a biological injury. We may become stuck in a state of what I call "chronic threat response" (CTR). CTR is not a diagnosis, and even people who do not meet criteria for a diagnosis of PTSD may have chronic threat response. CTR describes a state of being where one filters everything – the world we navigate, and our relationships, through a sense of threat. Our fight or flight system is stuck in one gear, and we can't throttle down. In this state of mind and body, we do things we regret. We hurt those we love, and this burns us with shame.

And often, as in Michael's case, chronic threat response has a negative impact on our careers as well. When his co-workers struggled, and Michael had the thought "that doesn't sound like a problem to me" it was because he was locked into a state of chronic threat response. Everything was filtered through a lens of threat, and he was suffering from such personal, unaddressed trauma and moral injury, that he lost connection with compassion for a time.

If we fail to recognize that trauma is stealing from us, either in one act of "grand larceny" that takes our very soul for a time, or by making off with little pieces of the life we once enjoyed, we risk losing everything. We may find ourselves close to the end of a tunnel, suffocating in sheer darkness before we even realize that we are there.

7

ATTACKED

In this chapter, we'll go into the courtroom with Michael, in the trial that followed the fatal shooting. But first, since the news at the time didn't give the full story – and Michael and his peers were undefended in the court of public opinion, let's do it right this time. Here is the missing context that would have been helpful for everyone to understand before Michael and his fellow officer were subjected to four years of legal action.

***

On the night of December 27, 2012, when we arrived at the

apartment on Creekside Drive, we saw evidence of forced entry through a shattered window next to the front door. As a result, it seemed that the man with a butcher knife, attacking the couple who lived there, was an unknown intruder. It turns out that he wasn't either unknown or an intruder. But as police officers responding to the call we received from dispatch, we had no way of knowing it. Anthony Banta Jr., the assailant, was their roommate.

The apartment had three bedrooms. We would later come to understand that Mr. Banta lived in one of them and a male roommate and his girlfriend were in another. The girlfriend had been the source of the blood curdling screams. The reason? She and her boyfriend were barricaded in their bedroom while Mr. Banta was attempting to use the butcher knife to break through the door. It was Mr. Banta's second attack on them that evening.

The girlfriend reported and later testified in court that prior to the knife attack, she had been lying asleep next to her boyfriend on the bed, while he was playing video games. She was suddenly awakened by the sounds of someone gagging, and saw Mr. Banta straddled on top of her boyfriend, attempting to choke him to death. She and her boyfriend were able to forcefully push him out of the apartment together. He then shattered the window, re-entered the apartment, grabbed the butcher knife from the kitchen and attacked them again, with the butcher knife.

In our use of force training as police officers, at the very top of the threat spectrum is when a suspect engages in "life threatening assault or assault likely to cause great bodily harm." This is defined as follows: "Subject commits an attack using an object, a weapon, or body parts, such as hands, feet, elbows, knees, in such a manner that the officer reasonably believes the assault will result in serious injury or death." (Source: Walnut Creek Police Department Manual; DIRECTIVE NO. 03-09D)

When we arrived at the scene, and the screams had been silenced, our first thought was that the assailant had just stabbed and killed someone – or possibly two people, in the upstairs bedroom. The assailant stood on the landing outside the bedroom, his face sweating profusely with a strange, fixed gaze. There were 4 officers present at one point, all telling him to drop the knife, commands to which he was completely unresponsive to at first. He then responded by saying, "I don't give a f-ck," raised the knife over his head in a position of attack and rushed at us with the butcher knife." There were no protective barriers between us and him, and the assailant was close enough to cover the distance between us in about one second, either by charging at us or throwing the knife in his hand. This was the context of the fatal shooting.

***

15 million dollars. After the night of the fatal shooting, the assailant's family immediately sued the City of Walnut Creek and each of the officers who were present for a total of 15 million dollars.

As a result, I spent the next several years fighting for my life in federal court.

In those days, being involved in a fatal shooting did not mean that an officer(s) would be sued. For example, in the previous fatal shooting that had occurred in my department with another officer more than 12 years prior, no one was sued. Nowadays, if you work as an officer, and you're involved in a fatal shooting, in all likelihood, you'll be sued.

When the civil lawsuit was filed, the Walnut Creek city council held a closed session, without the other officers and me present, or represented by legal counsel. The purpose of this session was to decide whether it would use its resources to defend us in the trial. The legal defense fund that we pay into as police officers covers criminal defense, but it does not cover civil litigation. The family had filed a civil rights lawsuit in federal court. To not defend us would have left us exposed to the loss of our jobs and hundreds of thousands of dollars in legal fees. This would have meant financial ruin for all of us, and the families we support. Fortunately, after reviewing the facts of the case, the city decided it would defend us, and they hired the McNamara Law Firm where I met Noah Blechman, who became our attorney.

The trial became the center of my life for many years. Before the civil trial even went to court, my fellow officers and I had already completed a District Attorney's investigation, an Internal Affairs investigation and a Coroner's inquest. We'd given hours of testimonies – including 3 recorded, transcribed interviews.

But on top of these proceedings, the assailant's family had hired a team of 4 or 5 lawyers and pressed civil action. The initial phase of the legal case involved depositions (interviews to collect information from defendants) spaced out over a period of 4 years, one at a time, often several months apart. After weeks or months of not hearing anything, I'd get a call from Noah Blechman, my attorney, and he'd say, "Michael, we have another deposition coming up."

Every time I'd get one of these calls from Noah, my level of stress would go through the roof. Every scheduled deposition would kick off rounds of reviewing everything in the previous investigations because any inconsistency, even if I couldn't recall a single detail, could result in serious consequences.

In preparing for the fight of my life, I had to remember every gritty detail – including reviewing the images of Mr. Banta lying dead on the floor. I would get terrible nightmares, night after night. In this way, the trauma of the event was repeatedly seared into my memory. It took an unbearable toll on all of us, while we continued to do our jobs as police officers, responding to calls that sometimes involved risking our lives in our role as Protectors.

The depositions were held in a small conference room at the lawyers' office. There was a court reporter present to record every word I said. I had my lawyer Noah Blechman there, and there were 4 or 5 lawyers from the plaintiff's side, along with Mr. Banta's father, who showed up for every single deposition. The interviews were recorded with a huge video camera positioned straight across from my face. These depositions took all day. For eight hours straight, with one short break for lunch, I was asked to answer an endless stream of hostile questions while Mr. Banta's father was sitting directly in front of me, his eyes full of grief and rage.

The lawyers on the opposing side would do anything they could to try to discredit me in any way possible – looking for holes in my report or questioning my level of training and fitness for duty.

Meanwhile, in the court of public opinion, we had no way to defend ourselves. My fellow officers and I were not permitted to discuss matters of an active case. Yet, we were continually subjected to misrepresentation of the facts in the media coverage about the case. The media painted us as "keystone cops," who didn't know what we were doing, bumbling our way through the interaction, and literally physically tripping over each other.

For instance, here is a line from an article at the time, published in the local newspaper on September 15, 2016:

> "The lawsuit alleges that one officer fired in panic in reaction to officers tripping over themselves when they first saw Banta, and then the other officers followed. Questions lobbied to Sugrue…implied that the plaintiffs think officers may have planted the knife under Banta's body after the shooting.[7]"

---

7   Fraley, M. (2016, Sept 15). East Bay Times. Bay Area News Group. Walnut Creek officer describes killing 22-year-old man who threatened officers. Retrieved from https://www.eastbaytimes.com/2016/09/15/walnut-creek-officer-describes-killing-22-year-old-man-who-threatened-officers/

And here's another excerpt from a media report made by News 24/680 at the time:

> "Banta's parents sued the city of Walnut Creek, Sugrue, Ezard, and two other officers for 15 million – maintaining that the slightly built Banta posed no threat that night, that the officers initially fired in a panic.[8]"

We had no way to defend ourselves against this kind of false representation. We were dragged through the mud in the press with no way to set the record straight.

My attorney, Noah Blechman, argued to have the case dismissed based on "qualified immunity". "Qualified immunity" is granted when officers are determined to act in good faith, and in alignment with policing protection standards in the line of duty. As mentioned previously, the judge granted qualified immunity for the first round of shots. This effectively meant that two of the four officers who responded were no longer defendants in the civil trial. Now, it was only me and the other male officer who remained as defendants in

---

[8]   News 24/680. (2016, Sept 23). Walnut Creek, Four Police Officers Exonerated in 2012 Fatal Shooting. Retrieved from https://news24-680.com/2016/09/23/walnut-creek-four-police-officers-exonerated-in-2012-fatal-shooting/

the 15-million-dollar federal lawsuit. And the judge decided to bring the case to trial to review all of the evidence in public court.

I can't say for sure what the judge's motivations were in bringing the case to trial. What I can say is that at this time, there were several national media stories about misuse of force by officers. Even though the fatal shooting happened in 2012, the height of the trial was in 2016 – at a time when there was a huge media focus on 4 major national stories about controversial fatal shootings by police officers. Specifically, the deaths of Michael Brown, Eric Garner, Philando Castile, and Jamar Clark sparked national outrage and widespread protests, and fueled the Black Lives Matter movement. As a result, anti-police sentiment was surging across the country.

This anti-police sentiment showed up clear as day within the jury pool. The idea of having a jury is that you have a group of "peers" who weigh the evidence of a case, without bias, to determine a just outcome. A jury holds your life in their hands. There we were in court, my fellow officer and myself, facing a jury of "our peers" and what we actually saw was a bunch of people who really didn't want to be there – who would say and do _anything_ to get out of serving.

I've been in court to testify in drug cases many times over the years. There is something sacred to me about being in court. To me, going to court is a solemn occasion. You dress professionally and you treat it with respect. I saw sitting across from me a group of people wearing t-shirts and shorts who were coming up with every excuse in the book to get out of serving jury duty.

During jury selection, this question was asked of the jury: "How many of you feel that police officers shouldn't carry handguns?"

About 1/3 of the jury pool raised their hands.

I wanted to throw up. My life is on trial and the people on the jury have no understanding of the kinds of dangers we face in the line of duty.

Most of the time, I was alone in that courtroom by myself, being treated like a common criminal. Other officers had fired shots, but forensics had determined that Officer Ezard and I had fired the lethal shots, so the focus was often on us.

To help you understand what this feels like, I need to paint the picture.

A full jury panel sits at close range, staring at me for hours a day. A parade of expert witnesses hired by the plaintiff comes in with a wide variety of baseless theories, calling us cold-blooded murderers in the open courtroom. The plaintiff's team of lawyers says all kinds of crazy things – that maybe he wasn't armed with a knife, that maybe we planted it on him, that even with a knife, he was not a real threat to us, that we were falling and tripping all over ourselves and that is why we shot him. They argue – to a jury including several people who didn't think we should carry handguns - that we shot a defenseless, unarmed man because we were incompetent.

And the family members are there every single day, including the identical twin brother of the man I killed. He's there too, sitting right behind me the whole time.

Can you imagine? This is the same face I've seen in my nightmares for the last four years. I can't get his face out of my head. It's now physically in the courtroom with me. During breaks in the courtroom proceedings, as we're walking down the hallway, his brother and other family members are giving us cold death stares and mumbling "murderers" under their breath. Every day that I sat in that courtroom, I was attacked – my training, my motivations, my competence, and my character - all were repeatedly attacked.

At the same time, I was going through a divorce, which brought another simultaneous legal battle into my life, and which ultimately cost me hundreds of thousands of dollars to resolve.

And then there is the fact that my dad, Mike Gormley, who was my strongest ally, the person who always had my back, died of cancer during the same year. Explaining the importance of this loss needs its own chapter.

The toll of all this combined is impossible to put into words.

Some people question whether the mind and body are connected. I don't. It's clear to me that emotional stress is directly connected to physical health problems. During 2015 and 2016, I had 16 biopsies on my face and body and 8 of them were cancerous, so in addition to the federal trial, and the divorce proceedings, I had to have 3 procedures to remove cancers on my face.

As the case dragged on, the city offered to settle with the assailant's family for $500,000. I understand that it was a business decision, but it really bothered me. I wanted it to be clear that we did our jobs. I didn't want to settle. I didn't want it to look like we did anything wrong. I was there on December 27, 2012. I knew we had done our jobs and I wanted proof, on the record, that we did the right thing.

Mr. Banta's family refused the settlement offer in any case.

In the end, there was no clarity on why Mr. Banta had suddenly, savagely attacked the couple he lived with. The pathologist offered three possible explanations for Mr. Banta's behavior: He took a designer drug that is not detectable on even the most sophisticated toxicology tests, he had an undiagnosed mental illness, or he suffered from a form of marijuana-induced psychosis that has been noted in medical literature in the past decade. Grieving the loss of their son, and without a clear explanation for his behavior, his family needed someone to blame.

But the thing is that I can't blame them. I really can't. Right or wrong, I took a life. I took a life and now I have to live with that.

We eventually got to the end of the trial. All the witnesses had been interviewed. All the groundless theories of the plaintiff's team of lawyers had been put forth. The paid expert witnesses for the plaintiff's side had attempted to shore up these theories.

On Friday, September 22, the jury went in to deliberate on the outcome. The jury asked to review some extra pieces of evidence during their deliberation. I had a really bad feeling about it. My stomach was in knots and my legs were shaking uncontrollably under the table. If the jury did not come in with their verdict by the end of the day, we'd have to wait for a whole weekend to get the verdict. Within the final hours of the day, the verdict came back.

We were found _not guilty of any wrongdoing._

I broke down sobbing in the open courtroom. I was beyond exhausted. Yet within 30 minutes of the verdict, I asked my lawyer Noah Blechman to ask the plaintiff's attorneys if I could have a private word with Mr. Banta's father. I wanted to tell him that I knew his son was not a bad person as far as the life he had lived before the night of the assault, and I was truly sorry that his son had died. His father refused to speak to me.

In his concluding comments, the judge, who happened to be the brother of a Supreme court justice, said that had it not been for our actions that night, more lives would have been lost.

We prevailed, but there were no winners.

All I could think of at the end of that trial was that I wanted to talk to the father of the man I killed. I wanted him to know that I was a human, that I didn't want this to happen, that I had no choice. And that, like him, I am a father who loves my child.

To this day, if he ever happens to listen to any of my interviews or anything I ever do, I just want to talk to that man and let him know. I don't know if I'll ever get the chance, and it weighs heavily on me.

Doc Springer's Reflections

This was the hardest chapter for me to write. It wasn't because of writer's block – it's because I hit a wall of anger several times in thinking through how to approach this particular chapter.

In preparing to write this chapter, I reviewed all of it – the recording of the coroner's inquest, Michael's depositions, transcriptions of the courtroom proceedings, local news reports at the time, the official policing standards maintained by the Walnut Creek police department, even the photos of the deceased assailant, lying curled at the bottom of a flight of stairs, with a pool of blood gathering beneath him.

Michael is not my patient. He's my friend. I know his heart, and his character. I know that he is the Phoenix Raven who was stoic despite cracked ribs during his final training test. I know that his deepest values are grounded in being a Protector and a Defender of what is right and just. I know that this was not a case of bumbling officers. With his background as a Raven, and hundreds of hours of tactical training in the police force, Michael is one of the most highly trained law enforcement officers I know.

As a patrol sergeant, Michael was responsible for ensuring that all the police officers on the street were properly trained.

During the proceedings, Michael was very vulnerable, in ways that are especially challenging for people who serve in military and policing roles. For instance, in the Coroner's Inquest, here are two excerpts - exact quotes - of how he described the threat that faced him and his fellow officers on the night of December 27:

"As I waited, I actually saw his hand come forward and I could see that it was a knife. It was a very large knife. And again, I've never seen a blue knife before. I was confused. But there was no mistake that I could see the blade and it was a very large blade. I'm not talking about a steak knife, a regular kitchen knife. This was a butcher-sized knife. And as he had that, again, myself and Officer Connors both have our guns pointed directly at him, both giving repeated, repeated [sic] commands, "Drop the knife, drop the knife." No response. This guy is staring right through us. Eyes have not moved, wide open. Dripping sweat. I have to tell you, in my combined years in the military and being a police officer, I have never once seen a person look like this as they [sic] did at me. And I have to tell you, a grown man, I was scared for my life. It's hard for me to sit here and even say that with what I do. People look to me to save lives. And we have to run towards danger, not run away from it….What caused me to react is, again, with the same look in his eye, there's no change in this guy's facial features at all. He comes up over with the knife and says, 'I don't give a fuck' and starts coming at us. At that point, I fired my weapon. All I could think about was I'm going to get stabbed and my partner is going to get stabbed."

As I pushed through and finished writing this chapter, I now understand why I hit these walls of anger. I felt angry because someone I know to fundamentally be a Protector – someone I care about as a personal friend - was so baselessly attacked over so many years. As I read the depositions, I saw how the team of lawyers hired to discredit Michael and his fellow officer joked around amongst each other, making a sport of it, while he was fighting for his life.

I saw evidence that they attacked him in any way they could, using words to attempt to trick him or trip him up. For example, at the start of one deposition, they asked Michael to explain his background and training, to which he says this (exact quote):

"I was in the military, active duty, for approximately six and a half years. During that time, I was promoted to the rank of Captain. I held various assignments including flight leader, flight commander, senior watch officer, officer recruiter, chief of security forces. While in the military, I completed several advanced courses that dealt with law enforcement anti-terrorism force protection, including FBI courses."

Throughout the proceedings, Michael is then asked questions like:

- Had you ever received any training that when you're approaching a dwelling with the window broken out, loud screams had been coming and all of a sudden they stopped and you believe someone was seriously injured, that you should stand right in front of a window before you enter?"

- "Have you ever been trained in using a flashlight attached to your gun as you approach a crime scene?"

- "Have you ever received training from the Walnut Creek

Police Department that whether or not you believe a suspect is alive or dead, that you need to disarm them as soon as possible?"

These kinds of questions are designed to compel a defendant to acknowledge what would appear to be "gaps" in training to an un-informed jury. This is done by posing extremely narrow, highly specific training scenarios, while military and police officer training is designed flexibly to allow for a response in fluid or "kinetic" environments. Michael, however, held his center throughout these repeated attacks, clarifying continually that he has been trained on numerous different scenarios and types of calls as part of his training and on the job experience.

At other times, during the depositions or court proceedings, opposing attorneys attempted to directly plant false and damaging information into the record to destroy Michael's credibility.

Here is a run of questioning around his shooting ability (the following excerpts are exact quotes from the legal proceedings).

Plaintiff's attorney: In the Walnut Creek Police Department, you have to go through qualifications every so often as an officer with your weapon, correct?

Michael: Yes.

Plaintiff's attorney: How many times a year do you have to do that qualification?

Michael: At least twice a year.

Plaintiff's attorney: And during that training, you have to have a certain percentage of accuracy, don't you?

Michael: Well, there's a certain number of times that you have to hit the target in a specified target area, yes.

Plaintiff's attorney: And the times you have been in 2012 to the firing range qualifications prior to this incident, you had very low marks, correct?

Michael: What do you mean "very low marks?"

Plaintiff's attorney: You barely hit the target.

Michael: I don't understand what you're asking me.

Plaintiff's attorney: Well, that what was your percentage of targets that were hit? You said you had to have a certain percentage where you hit the target, right?

Michael: No, I didn't say that. What I said was that in our qualifications we have to hit the target in certain areas in a specified area.

Plaintiff's attorney: And you had problems doing that, correct?

Michael: No.

At various times throughout the interview, the opposing attorneys showed that their "knowledge" of policing is based on movies and television shows. For example, they ask Michael if he is a "sharp shot" and he responds, "There's no sharp shot. What's a sharp shot?" or they refer to an officer having a "service revolver" to which Michael clarifies that the police officers who serve and protect us (i.e., those who take real risks, rather than those who portray officers on gumshoe detective shows of the 1970s) don't actually carry revolvers.

The opposing lawyers attacked Michael by continuing to plant false ideas into the proceedings. They even attempted to bait Michael by comparing him to the character of Barney, a bumbling detective in a television show of their era who was played by Don Knotts. Here is a specific example from the official transcripts:

Plaintiff's attorney: Okay. And as far as you can recall, you don't have a tremor in your wrist when you're shooting do you?

Michael: What do you mean 'a tremor'?

Plaintiff's attorney: Your hand is not shaking. You know, sometimes, no disrespect, but sometimes Barney Fife is holding a gun and shaking; you don't do that, do you?

Michael: I don't have any condition that I'm aware of where I shake my wrist.

They asked him questions that are so off-the-wall that I would imagine they are thrown into the mix to see if they can shake him. For example,

Plaintiff's attorney: Okay. Had you ever learned that Anthony Banta has been a health food fanatic?

Michael: No, I didn't know that.

Plaintiff's attorney: And had you ever learned that he had been someone that ate a lot of broccoli and other things?

Michael: I had no idea what he ate or didn't eat.

As Michael later explained to me, the opposing attorneys were suggesting that a docile Banta was in fact chopping leafy green vegetables, in stark opposition to the sworn testimony of his roommates that he attempted to murder them - testimonies given by people who hugged and thanked Michael for saving their lives after Banta was taken out.

The plaintiff's attorneys even attempted to split Michael from his fellow officers. This was the only part of the transcripts that caused me to smile, instead of hitting a wall of anger.

The prosecution asked Michael if he is faster than the female officer who responded alongside him on the night of December 27.

Plaintiff's attorney: Can you run faster than her?

Michael: I don't know. We've never raced.

In a particularly revealing line of inquiry, one of the opposing attorneys cast himself in the role of a television "gumshoe" detective when he referred to himself as "Columbo."

Michael's attorney, Noah Blechman, asked an opposing attorney, "How much more do you have with this witness?" and the attorney responded, "Probably a little bit more. Maybe like Columbo, a little bit."

Blechman responded, "Yeah, I don't know what that is exactly but…"

And the same opposing side attorney said, "Columbo always has just one more question."

Columbo, for those unfamiliar, is a television "gumshoe" detective with a glass eye played by Harry Falk in the 1970s. To use the old-timey language these opposition lawyers seem to favor, Columbo has a predictable "schtick" that goes as follows. He asks a series of easy questions that a fictionalized killer answers easily, whereafter he seems to wrap up the conversation, and then brings up "one more thing" that catches the killer in a damning lie, resulting in a criminal conviction. So, in referencing himself as "Columbo" this lawyer was likely posturing in a narcissistic way – letting Michael and his attorney think he had an ace up his sleeve (he didn't).

With the other statements above, this shows the mentality of the individuals on the plaintiff's legal team, who were unleashed on Michael for four years. As further confirmation, if you go to the California State Bar Association, and look up the head lawyer, Anthony Ngula Luti (license #207852) of the Luti Law Firm, which represented Mr. Banta's family, you'll see that he has been permanently disbarred from practicing law[9].

---

9   https://apps.calbar.ca.gov/attorney/Licensee/Detail/207852

This is the official statement you'll find:

Anthony Ngula Luti #207852

License Status: Disbarred

This licensee is prohibited from practicing law in California by order of the California Supreme Court.

Address: The Luti Law Firm, 7095 Hollywood Blvd Ste 351, Hollywood, CA 90028

Scroll down the page and you'll notice multiple disciplinary actions, beginning in 6/13/2013, when his license was first suspended to his official disbarment on 1/18/2019. The 2013 sanction means that Mr. Luti lost his license to practice law for a time and was then subsequently disbarred. Disbarment is the most serious penalty a lawyer can receive. Disbarred attorneys are publicly identified on the website of their state's bar association. A disbarred attorney who continues to practice law can be charged with a misdemeanor or even a felony in some cases. A potential felony jail sentence for this offense can be as long as three (3) years.

_____

(accessed 1/2/2021)

The other thing I need to address, from a more dispassionate perspective, as a psychologist, is that the settlement offer is a particularly insidious kind of moral injury. Michael understood that it was the city making a business decision. As so often happens in law and politics, the involved parties sometimes offer deals just to end the prolonged trauma and/or cost of a lawsuit. Michael certainly had no part or control in that decision.

But imagine encountering someone with a deadly weapon, who was unresponsive to your efforts to de-escalate the threat. Imagine how it would feel to have someone attack you, and people you are sworn to protect, with a butcher knife. Imagine that you acted in a way that is fully and appropriately aligned with use-of-force policy and standard practice for your profession. Imagine that while you acknowledge the trauma of having to take a life, you also know in your heart and soul that what you did saved lives. Imagine that you had acted on an inviolable personal right to defend yourself against a potentially lethal injury – a right that is never forfeit – even for those who serve in our military or LEO communities.

And then imagine that someone else gets a payout that makes you look guilty of wrong-doing and that this settlement is publicly recorded? This is a serious moral injury – not just a "trauma," but a deep wound to the soul. Ultimately, Michael and his fellow officers were cleared of any wrongdoing, but the offer of a settlement was a moral injury.

8

MY DAD

Michael's dad, Mike Gormley, is a local legend in one of the grittiest police departments in the Bay Area. One of the best ways to get to know someone is to ask their co-workers about them. This chapter starts with two stories, shared by Mike Gormley's fellow officers. The first story comes from an interview with a K9 officer who served beside Mike for many years, and the second from another fellow officer. After that, Michael speaks to the importance of his relationship with his dad, Mike Gormley.

***

From a K9 officer who served with Mike Gormley:

"I've been a dog person all my life. I know that there is no 'bad breed.' For example, sometimes people think that pit bulls are instinctively aggressive, but I've seen pit bulls that are extremely gentle, even with little children. Pit bulls, like any dog, can be shaped by their owners. And because they have a huge jaw that can do serious damage, they are the breed of choice for many of the drug dealers who train them to guard their stash.

When Mike and I were working together, I was the K9 officer with a trained dog who would identify where illegal drugs were being stored. I had a beautiful Belgian Malinois helping me. Together, we were so effective that the local drug dealers eventually put a hit out on me. So, when we went to places where drug dealers were, I had to have a sizable escort, protection from several officers guarding the street in both directions while we did our searches.

One day, we were at this drug dealer's house looking for the drugs, with 20 officers providing back up. Our search of the house yielded nothing. But then as we were exiting the house, my dog locked in on the car that was parked out front. She started to get excited as she sniffed under the back bumper of the car, around the tailpipe area.

Over the fence was the biggest pit bull I've ever seen – about 120 pounds. The pit bull was getting amped up as my dog was closing in on the drugs. Suddenly the pit bull visually locked onto me, jumped over a 6-foot fence, and came charging at me at full speed. Of the 20 officers who were there to protect me, none of them, other than Mike, did so. They all jumped back and got clear of the pit bull's charge. I turned toward the attack and put my foot out in front of me. The pit bull hit me with such force that I went down, flat on my back. The pit bull had my right foot in its mouth, biting down hard while I lay defenseless on my back.

My dog, who weighed half as much as the pit bull, turned on the pit bull to protect me. The pit bull let go of my right foot and lunged at my dog, locking on its throat with its massive jaw, crushing the larynx of my beautiful dog.

It was then that Mike Gormley walked up to me and said, "are you ready?" He was the only one in all of those officers who stepped into the fray, with a calm, collected voice. He was warning me that he was going to shoot the pit bull, so that I could protect myself and my dog. I wordlessly signaled to do it. Mike put his gun up to the chest of the pit bull and fired 3 rounds in succession, at an angle that would not endanger me, my dog, or any other person in the area. The pit bull released my dog's throat, ran away from us for a few paces, and then turned around and charged us again. I was still lying on my back, totally defenseless. My dog was on the ground as well, blood flowing from her neck. Mike stepped over us, and shot the pit bull one more time, this time killing it.

My dog was rushed to the ER on a code 3 run. She was eventually saved but came close to being killed that day. The drug dealer told us that he was really sorry and that if he had known that his dog could jump the fence, he would have tied him up. That was one of 7 times I was attacked by pit bulls during my time as a K9 officer. It was the time I came closest to being badly injured or killed myself. Mike Gormley was the only officer out of 20 officers present who was willing to protect me in such a dangerous encounter. That's who Mike was – and that's why he became so widely respected within the police force."

Another fellow officer said this about Mike.

"Mike told me that when I went over to his son Michael's police department (in Walnut Creek), I should look in on his son. Well, I tried, but couldn't find anyone in that department who was named 'Michael Gormley.' So, I went back to Mike Gormley and told him that I couldn't find anyone with that last name. He said, "Oh, well, it's because he has a different last name. His last name is Sugrue.

But he's my son. Say hello to him next time you go there."

What follows is Michael's reflections on how his relationship with his dad shaped his life.

Many people go through an extended period to discover what they want to do with their lives.

I never did.

Ever since I was a kid, I had always wanted to be a police officer, just like my dad Mike Gormley, who was my hero, and protector from when I was young. While Mike was not my biological father, he was my dad. Here's how he came into my life.

My parents were married until I was eight years old. My biological father's best friend from high school was a man named Mike, who later went on to become a legend in the Richmond Police Department.

Mike was part of my life since the day I was born. He was always "Mike" and I was always "Michael."

A couple years after my parents divorced, Mike and my mom got married. This was a happy day that I will always remember. It was a huge wedding. Lots of family members from both sides were there.

Mike was already family to me, even before he married my mom. More than that in fact. I had always looked up to him – figuratively, and literally, since he stood at six feet, three inches.

When Mike married my mom, I was just a kid, and he was working for the Sausalito Police Department. Sausalito PD is where he brought me into the circle.

I started as a crime prevention volunteer. I got my own laminated ID card from the Sausalito Police Department. Initially, I'd go in and file pamphlets in the lobby, help Mike organize his desk, and wash patrol cars.

Some of you may remember "McGruff," the dog who was a mascot for crime prevention ("take a bite out of crime.") Every year, I'd ride with McGruff in the crime prevention parade in downtown Sausalito.

It was a very small, tight-knit department with a great feeling of camaraderie. I instantly felt like I was part of a family. That's when I really had my first desire to work in law enforcement.

To me, it wasn't a job. It was a family – a community, a group of people that belong together. Looking back, it's kind of funny talking about it, but that was a huge deal for me.

After my stepdad transferred to the Richmond Police Department, where he and my uncle both worked as officers, I was invited to join the police explorer program. To become a part of the program, we had to go through a background check and a formal application process. As "police explorers," we went through a week-long police academy for cadets in San Diego.

After completing the week-long cadet academy, the "police explorer" program was a regular part of my life with weekly meetings and trainings. We worked special events – for example, we worked parking details for the big fairs in Hercules and Richmond- helping direct traffic. We got a badge, which to me felt like being handed the Holy Grail. It was an actual metal police badge with a star insignia that said, "Richmond Police Explorer." We also wore a light blue uniform shirt with the same shoulder patch the police officers wore.

From very early in my life, I've always been interested in both the military and law enforcement. I had also been part of the Boy Scouts program and knew the feeling of belonging and accomplishment that comes with getting badges and patches.

Additionally, my maternal grandfather served in the Army Air Corps during World War II. I remember going to his house and seeing pictures of him in uniform. He showed me some of his medals. When my grandfather died, I was in college, in the Air Force ROTC program. I have a vivid memory of going to my grandfather's funeral in my full "dress uniform," with all my ribbons and medals.

When I got my first metal badge as a police explorer, I was already really drawn to the symbolic importance of that badge. In getting that badge, I felt accepted and part of something very special. Whether it was as a police explorer, a cub scout or a police volunteer, I felt like I was doing something to help make a difference. What motivated me even more was knowing how proud my parents were of all that I was doing, and it made me feel proud of myself too.

Even more than my grandfather, my stepdad, Mike Gormley, was the man I most wanted to make proud. Mike was the model of the man I wanted to become. In my heart, Mike Gormley is my dad.

During the end of my active-duty time in the Air Force, I was stationed back in California. My heart has always been in the Northern California Bay Area, so I applied to several local law enforcement agencies. I had been offered a job pending the background check process with Richmond Police Department

when I got a conditional job offers from Contra Costa County,
Sacramento Police Department and Walnut Creek
Police Department.

Part of me really wanted to work for Richmond PD, but part of me
had this sense that I wanted to make my own way. I guess I felt like
if I worked at Richmond PD, I'd always be in Mike's shadow
because he was a legend there. I already knew that my stepfather
loved me and that he was proud of me. But I often tell people that
I'm not half the cop he was.

When I was a kid, after my biological father and mother got
divorced, my biological father became financially successful. He
had his own business, fancy cars, a huge house in the Oakland
Hills, and a model girlfriend, then wife. Eventually, my biological
father got involved in drugs and alcohol and it got to a point where
his life started falling apart. We started distancing ourselves. I
would see him only occasionally, mostly living with Mike and my
mom.

Because of his addictions, my biological father wasn't reliable. I can
remember times when he was supposed to come pick me up and he
never showed up. After he died, my mom told me about other times
when he showed up intoxicated.

My mom told me that my stepfather took my father outside on one occasion. He told him that if he ever showed up like that again, that he was going to call the police. Even when I had no awareness, Mike was always my protector. He was the strong, reliable dad I needed.

As I said, Mike Gormley was a legend in his department. Over 240 pounds of muscle, and standing at 6', 3", he was kind, but he took care of business. He cared about his people. He spent most of his career working homicides, so he was always on call. For example, I can remember going out to dinner and the movies and we'd have to take two separate cars in case he got called out. Even though he was gone a lot, I always knew he had my back. Whenever I needed him, he would drop what he was doing. He showed up when I needed him most.

I remember one particular day when I was commuting to St. Mary's as a Freshman in high school in Berkeley. It was a long trip from where we were living at the time. Every day, I had to get up early, walk to a bus stop, take a bus to the subway (B.A.R.T.) station, take B.A.R.T., and then walk to school. And then do the whole commute in reverse at the end of the day.

While I was on the final thirty minute bus ride headed home, the last leg of my commute, a man started harassing me. He was in his late 20s or early 30s. He was disheveled and smelled strongly of alcohol. He was constantly staring at me as though trying to bait me into a fight.

I was hoping he would get off the bus before me, but when I got to my stop, he followed me off the bus. Rather than walking straight home, I ran to the closest pay phone and called Mike. He showed up almost immediately. I remember that Mike handed me his gun and said, "Wait right here."

Mike grabbed this man by his upper arms, almost lifting him off the ground, looked him straight in the eye and had words with him.

The look of absolute fear on the man's face was one that I'll never forget. I had never seen Mike do anything like this before, and I'll always vividly remember his presence and what he said to this guy. It was a powerful moment for me – a memory that solidified the feeling that Mike was my protector.

He did the same thing for me when I called him at 4 a.m. after the shooting on December 27, 2012. He immediately got in his car and drove 30 miles from Fairfield to Walnut Creek. He showed up in his suit. He looked me right in the eye and told me that everything was going to be okay. His presence and words brought an immediate sense of calm to me. Mike was always there when I needed him – after the shooting, when I was sued by the family, and when my marriage fell apart.

In the middle of all of it, Mike got diagnosed with stage four lung cancer. Shortly after his diagnosis, I was informed that my fellow officers and I would be given a formal award in relation to the night of the fatal shooting. Walnut Creek had not experienced an officer involved fatal shooting for over a decade, and when the last one occurred, it involved a running gunfight that ended in the death of an armed suspect. The officers involved had each been given a Medal of Valor award. In our case, we had run into a residence where an armed suspect was attempting to murder a couple and had shot him when he then attacked us.

As my dad was fighting for his life, he wasted away, becoming a shell of his former self. I knew that this medal ceremony would be the last one my dad would ever see. I also knew that seeing his son get the Medal of Valor would make him glow with pride. It would honor his role in my life, his continual investment in me, and lifelong example of what it means to be a Protector and Defender. Based on how my fellow officers and I had moved to protect an innocent couple, incurring serious risk to ourselves in the process, and in light of the previous Medal of Valor decision, I hoped and expected that this would be the outcome. It wasn't. Instead, I was informed that we would be awarded a Distinguished Service Medal. The reason? Here is exactly what I was told, "It was a dangerous situation, but it didn't rise to that level. You were all just doing your job."

My dad died 6 months after the award ceremony. When I lost him, I was not only grieving, but I felt totally alone during some of the worst traumas of my life.

I didn't have anybody I could fully trust that I could talk to about work-related stress. I trusted my mom and I talked to her about lots of things, but not about the job.

Throughout my entire career, Mike was always my mentor and role model. If I had an issue, a question, or a situation I was dealing with at work, I knew I could always go to him.

When I graduated from the police academy, Mike pinned my badge on me. I have a picture of it still to this day. He's looking at me with a look of pride. If a fire ever threatened my home, that's one of the first pictures I'd grab on my way out the door.

At the height of all my trauma, and at the lowest point in my life, I lost my hero, my protector, my dad.

Doc Springer's Reflections

The warrior spirit is about something much deeper than combat operations during wartime.

Sometimes I am asked, "How would you define a 'warrior'?" To me, a warrior is someone who:

- Dedicates him- or herself to a greater purpose,

- has clarity on the people and values they hold sacred, and,

- is willing to make substantial, ongoing, personal sacrifices to protect and defend these things.

Mike Gormley was a warrior in his own right. As his K9 officer colleague shared, he was the only officer out of a large group of officers who was willing to step into the fray when she was attacked. He was also continually on the spot when Michael needed him, even when Michael was not aware.

From a young age, Michael modeled his own warriorship on his father Mike's example. It was Mike who "brought him into the circle" of the LEO community. It was Mike who gave him practical opportunities to "test drive" a career in law enforcement. It was Mike who showed Michael an example of a leader who cares about his people – who is willing to risk his life for them if needed.

For both Mike Gormley and Michael Sugrue, their work as LEO professionals is not a "job," but rather a "calling." This feeling of being "called" is relatively common among those who serve as Protectors and Defenders – whether in the military or law enforcement professions. Some individuals, like Michael, show interest in warrior paths from a very early age. For others, their warriorship may come into full awareness as they take on their professional identities.

Once a person connects with his or her warrior identity and joins a "Tribe" of fellow warriors, it's impossible to go back. Exercising warriorship is integrated into one's daily life. Warriors do not have "co-workers" – they have "brothers" and "sisters" in the new families they create. As they become accepted into these new families, they risk their lives for each other, which bonds them irreversibly. Warriorship and membership in the Tribe becomes a matter of one's core identity.

For this reason, the loss of a job is not just the loss of a job – it's the loss of one's identity, and the family that has been created. These world-altering losses – or the fear of them if one were to be sidelined, is one of the reasons why we are losing many of our strongest, bravest citizens to suicide. The occupation-identity link is one of the greatest overlooked vulnerabilities of our military servicemembers and first responders. Whereas people who pursue a wide variety of civilian occupations can "re-invent" themselves with relative ease, it's a different story for many who serve in military or first responder occupations. When Michael speaks of his fear of losing "everything" because of the trial that followed the fatal shooting – he was not just referring to financial ruin, or loss of a job. He was referring to the loss of his identity and his two families – his wife and daughter, and his law enforcement family. And the loss of both was tied to Mike Gormley's sudden death – since Mike represented both families in one person.

Mike Gormley's death made Michael much more psychologically vulnerable than he had been. Mike was Michael's primary father figure, and he was Michael's ultimate protector during the worst moments of his life. Mike Gormley was a rare, larger-than-life kind of individual – this was confirmed by his colleagues. Michael is not exaggerating when he says that Mike Gormley was a "legend" in the Richmond police department. Mike was unusually tall. He weighed over 200 pounds, solid muscle, with broad shoulders, and sufficient strength to lift a grown man off the ground to bring him up to his own eye level. And he looks like Tom Selleck in the role of Magnum P.I. (Take a look for yourself – Michael and I posted a picture of him on our website page about the book – on www.docshaunaspringer. com).

Over the course of just a few months, Michael watched his protector waste away from the ravages of cancer. Imagine the helplessness of…

- Being sued for millions of dollars

- Being unable to defend yourself when the press published false and damning allegations

- Being forced to sit through days of depositions and trial proceedings

- Going through a divorce and losing access to your child

- Getting 16 biopsies, eight of which were determined to be cancerous

- Suddenly losing your dad, who was the only person you could talk to about everything else…

All at the same time.

9

RECKLESS PURSUIT

One of the curious truths about human nature is that we're not very good at predicting how we're going to feel in the future. Lottery winners, new husbands and brides, those who receive a Nobel Peace Prize, may be surprised by their own emotional reactions. What about someone who has been under attack for 4 years, that has finally been declared "not guilty?"

In this chapter, Michael takes us through the days and months just after the end of the trial.

***

As the trial stretched painfully over so many years, a single thought formed in my mind. If I could just hold on, we would be exonerated, and it would all stop. I could put this behind me and move on, once I had been declared not guilty of any wrongdoing.

I clung to this vision and persisted because of it. This was the voice of "hope."

This vision turned out to be a mirage in a desert of endless pain.

When the judgment came in, I broke down, sobbing in the open courtroom.

My next thought arose with urgency: "I have to talk to Mr. Banta's father. I need to tell him how sorry I am that his son is gone. Before he walks out of this room, I must make sure he knows that this has affected me personally, in a major way."

As I mentioned previously, he would not speak to me. In fact, in the weeks to come, I would learn that Mr. Banta and his legal team immediately appealed the judgment and pressed forward with further litigation.

On the day of the judgment, everyone on my legal defense team was genuinely happy about the outcome. I definitely felt a wave of relief, but no happiness. Why was I not feeling happy?

There's a picture of me that was taken just after the judgment came in, to commemorate our victory. You can take a look at it on the website page about the book (www.docshaunaspringer.com). In the picture, I'm standing with some of my colleagues in the Police Department, along with my lawyer and his legal assistant. You can see that there's no joy or happiness on my face. I'm smiling but feeling nothing, other than sheer exhaustion. After years of attacks, I was totally spent.

On the final day of the trial, the Chief of Police and my Captain showed up. After the judgment came in, they told us that they were proud of us. My department immediately issued a press release to establish that we had been exonerated. That night, the Chief and Captain personally took us out to a nice dinner in San Francisco at a high-quality steakhouse. They put us up in a nice hotel so that we could relax and enjoy the evening without worrying about driving home. During the dinner the mood was jovial, and the food was delicious. *Why could I not feel genuinely happy?*

 Looking back, after our conversations during this project, I now understand that my nervous system had been shot after years of chronically acute stress. As a result, I could feel only certain specific emotions – anger or fear, or nothing at all, but numbness.

After dinner, a small group of us formed a single thought: Let's go out and get completely wasted. We felt like we had earned this. Personally, I wanted to get so drunk that I would be able to forget all of it - even for a few hours. And then wake up the next day with a sense of starting a new chapter.

Alcohol promises this kind of relief and release, but this was just another false hope. We did get out-of-our-mind drunk. Somehow, I got separated from the group and found myself walking through the Tenderloin District, San Francisco's skid row, at 3 am. The shops had heavy steel bars on them to prevent people from breaking the windows and stealing their inventory. The streets smelled of urine. Homeless people wrapped in oily blankets slept on the urine-stained sidewalk. Prostitutes walked by, trying to catch my eye. I was all alone, walking down skid row, completely intoxicated, and totally defenseless, wearing a nice business suit.

I tried calling my friends. The first three did not answer. The fourth one picked up the phone and immediately said, "Where are you, Michael?" I tried to describe my location, but the phone reception kept cutting out. Two bars, one bar, then no reception at all. A feeling of panic welled up as I realized my state of vulnerability. I could not bring help. In that environment, and in my drunken state, I was the definition of "easy prey."

Eventually, I flagged down a cab and told him the name of my hotel. In my alcohol and panic-soaked brain, I felt fearful that the cab driver might kidnap me and take my wallet. I was that defenseless. Fortunately, he dropped me off at my hotel. I stumbled into my room, collapsed on the bed, and blacked out.

A few hours later, I was awakened by the vibration of my phone in my pocket. As my phone screen came to life, I saw that I had missed more than 20 calls from my mother.

I called her immediately and heard primal fear in her voice: "Michael where have you been?!! It's your brother! He's in the ICU and I don't think he's going to make it."

A tidal wave of panic swept over me. With my head throbbing, I grabbed my things, threw them in a bag, and drove more than an hour to get to the hospital as soon as I could.

I found my brother hooked up to several tubes, lying still in a medically induced coma. My life had become a continual living nightmare.

Two days later, I went back to work because I didn't have any vacation days to draw from. While on the job, I was operational - projecting the image of myself as strong and capable. At work, I felt invincible.

At home, the nightmare continued. It was relentless. My dreams tortured me with thoughts of what could have happened. The plaintiff's lawyers tried their best to portray alternative versions of reality to support their attacks. For example, they argued that despite the sworn testimony of his roommates, the call to 911 and the bedroom door hanging off its hinges, maybe a harmless Banta was only chopping some broccoli for his vegetarian dinner... or... maybe the officers arrived, and tripped over each other, causing an accidental misfire that killed Banta, and then they all decided to cover it up. These stories distort reality, but they have a strategic purpose. They are designed to be emotionally compelling and lead jurors to envision that wrongful action was done.

All the crazy theories I had been subjected to over the past several years by my attackers played at my mind, especially at nighttime. They planted the seed of imagining what "might've been" if time and circumstance had been slightly altered. What if Mr. Banta had simply dropped the knife? Then nothing that followed would have happened. My life would not have been derailed. I would have continued to advance through the ranks in my job. I would not have lost my marriage. I would be living with my wife and raising our beautiful daughter in our dream home. The torture of the trial and all those depositions would never have happened.

After the trial was over, I felt even more tortured. The hope of feeling relief from the judgment was clearly a false one. During months of sleepless nights, my mind played tricks on me, giving me visions of an alternate path in my dreams, Banta dropping the knife, only to awake and find that my life was a continual living nightmare. I started to drink more, and I got to a place where I didn't care if I lived or died.

It's kind of hard to explain this, but I had a strong fear of death while at the same time, I didn't care if I died. The fear of death had settled deep into me during the night of the knife attack by Mr. Banta. In the years that followed, this fear was stoked by the loss of my father to lung cancer, my repeated diagnoses and treatments for my own skin cancer, and the trauma of nearly losing my brother the day after the trial. Death had infiltrated my defenses. I felt like it was inevitable that I would die.

When I was not on duty, I was consumed by this single run of thoughts: *I'm going to die, and my daughter will forget me. She will never know how much I love her. My ex-wife will wipe my existence out of her memory. She will move on as though I never existed in her life. And whoever my ex-wife marries will be the only father that my daughter knows or remembers.*

These thoughts became so paralyzing that my only relief from them was to take multiple selfies with my daughter every time I visited her. I would take at least four or five pictures of the two of us and then post it to my social media accounts. It was an insurance policy against the thoughts that tortured me. I figured that if I created a record, in a public place on my social media accounts, someday my daughter might get curious and find all those pictures and know that she was deeply loved by me, her dad.

When I was at work, I had a totally different mindset. When I was at work, I felt no fear at all. It was a strange mix of feeling invincible, as though nothing could touch me after what I had just survived, and also not caring if I died. My suicidality coalesced into this thought: *If I die in the line of duty, I will be memorialized forever and there will be no way that my daughter will forget me.*

I started to act on this thought by doing reckless things that endangered myself, and my fellow officers. The first incident was when we got a call at a problem house on the border of our town and the next town over. This house had been taken over by drug dealers and had become a flophouse for addicts. The call came in that there was a disturbance, and someone heard screaming.

Without conscious thought, I jumped in my patrol car, turned on the siren, and drove to the house as fast as I could. There were officers already in place, huddled in a small group that were strategizing how to make a safe entry. The house was two stories tall, and full of any number of addicts and criminals, some of whom were likely to be armed.

Without care or caution, and against all my training, I ran straight into the residence. I was driven by a blinding rage. I didn't care who was in there or if they were armed. By running into the house, I forced my fellow officers to back me up and put their lives in danger as a result. In that dangerously suicidal state of mind, I was absolutely a liability to my fellow officers.

Somehow by sheer good luck, no one was injured as a result of my reckless pursuit. A fellow supervisor, someone I respect, who is a defensive tactics expert, pulled me aside and confronted me with strong words when the scene had been secured.

I was still out of my mind with rage. He was 100% right and I was 100% wrong. I'm embarrassed to admit that I shamed him for being too scared to go into the house. I drove a rift between us. He never reported my reckless action or how I had handled his confrontation of it. In a way, I was glad that he didn't report it. At the same time, on some level, I wish he had. I think that if he had reported it, and someone up the chain had asked me about it, I might have broken down and talked about how I was not OK.

The second incident came a couple months later when I made a traffic stop on the freeway. Freeway stops are always dangerous. Typically, officers will use their PA system to have cars exit the freeway so that they can pull them over off the freeway. Without conscious thought, I pulled over a speeding car on the shoulder of a high-speed freeway. With freeway traffic rushing by at 70+ mph, as I was walking from the patrol car to the other car, I had this sudden rush of thoughts:

It would be so easy for me to just step backwards. One or two steps backward and it would be all over. All the pain and the suffering. I would be killed in the line of duty. This would solve all my problems. My daughter would get a financial pay out and would remember me forever as a hero.

I shook the thought off and completed the traffic stop but that thought clung to me, calling to me in the back of my mind.

The third incident showed how suicidal I really was. A few months later, I was sitting in the downtown office with another sergeant and a call came in: "There is a subject with a knife at a local department store, cutting the security cables on expensive items in the electronics department."

I heard the word KNIFE. It seared into my mind, bringing me straight back to the memory of the shooting on December 27. I got a mental picture of a crazy guy with a knife. Banta's face appeared in my mind. Without conscious thought or decision, I ran to my patrol car, jumped in, and floored it, driven by my demons. I wanted to get there before anyone else did, before there was any back up.

We are trained to carefully assess a situation and make a tactical plan before confronting a subject, especially one we know to be armed. All that training went out the window. People sometimes talk about death by cop. The opposite also applies. Police officers who are in a suicidal mind state can also use criminals as their means to act on their wish to die.

 As my patrol car came in at high speed, I saw a man who matched the subject's description come out of the bushes around the side of the store. Against all my training, I stopped the patrol car a few feet from him, jumped out and pulled my weapon on him. I cornered him and forced a confrontation, with no back up and no way of escaping.

I told him to put his hands in the air. In response, he stared at me with the same crazy look I had seen on the face of Mr. Banta. Instead of putting his hands in the air, he reached one hand into his pocket. Adrenaline dumped into my system, bringing a hyper-focus on his hand, holding the handle of a large knife. I could see the knife slowly emerging from his pocket. KNIFE! My brain screamed and my muscles responded. My finger slid to the trigger of my firearm, and I ordered him, "Drop the knife or I'm going to shoot you!!"

While we were locked on each other, neither of us moving, another patrol car arrived, and a fellow officer dismounted - my back up. Only then did the man drop the knife. My fellow officers apprehended and secured him. After he was put in handcuffs, they found that he was fully armed and very dangerous. He was a hardened criminal with a rap sheet 30 pages long.

They discovered that he had 8 knives in his possession, some of which he was hiding in other pockets. If backup had not arrived, it is likely he would have attacked me with one of the many knives he was carrying. The most likely scenario is this. He would have dropped the knife in his hand. I would then have holstered my weapon. And he would have taken another one of many concealed knives and attacked me.

This dangerous encounter should have been a wake-up call to me. But the truth is that in my altered state of mind, even this brush with death was not the wake-up call that pulled me out of my suicidal spiral.

That wake-up call came two months later through my best friend, John Davison.

Doc Springer's Reflections

In the field of psychology, we often treat suicidality as though it were fairly uncomplicated. Either you have a wish to die, or you don't.

The questions that most mental health providers ask are based on this straightforward, linear predictive model. Various training outfits have made a lot of money from packaging questions that make the assumption of a fixed mind state - either you are suicidal, or you are not.

Questions like, "Do you have any thoughts of harming yourself" or "Do you have a plan to end your life?" are the way that many providers currently assess suicidality. When a patient says "no" to these kinds of questions, many providers try to conceal their sigh of relief. They document that they've done an assessment and the patient is "not a risk to him or herself."

And here's a really critical insight - <u>many providers (and people in general) interpret statements about the fear of death as an indication that someone wants to preserve their life.</u>

Is it possible for someone to have a fear of death and to be deeply suicidal at the same time?

YES. I've seen this puzzling phenomenon fairly often at the end of the tunnel of despair. And it makes sense at some level, if we move beyond simple thinking, and fully integrate the complexity of a suicidal mind.

The suicidal mind state is one of profound disconnection. It is an altered state of reality. Nearly everything in human nature, other than that which is caused by active psychosis, has a "logic," but sometimes it is a complicated logic. It is not the simple, concrete, and ultimately false logic that drives our current assessment and interventional practices.

I was recently watching a powerful documentary film organized by Mission 22. In this film, there is a veteran named Olga who is rebuilding her life with support from Mission 22's innovative "Recovery and Resiliency" program. In the film, she reflects on the start of her healing journey before she began to heal. She gives words to the profound sense of helplessness that had consumed her previously.

As she puts it, "I didn't want to hurt myself, but I couldn't help wanting to hurt myself." This single statement perfectly encapsulates just how complex suicidality can be. At one level, people may not want to die. They may even have a terrifying fear of death, yet, at another level, they may feel relentlessly hunted by their demons. For a thorough understanding of the suicidal mode, and mind state, I would suggest reading my previous book, WARRIOR: How to Support Those Who Protect Us. For the present purposes, I'll share that when the voice of despair is strong, it creates the feeling that suicide is the only logical solution for one's problems.

Related to this, here is another critical point. Michael was never "suicidal" when he was off work. He never actively formed a plan to take himself out. If he talked about his fear of death, his therapist might have assumed this indicated a strong will to live. In all likelihood, they would have worked on his fear of death, and missed the risk of suicide entirely – both of them.

If his therapist had gone down the path of asking him, "Do you have any suicidal thoughts?" he would have said "no." Further, if his therapist had asked him if he had any past or current plans to harm himself, he would have again said "no" in all honesty.

Because this scenario has played out so many times with the veterans and first responders that I serve, I imagine he also might have added for good measure, "I love my daughter and I would never want to do that to her."

All these responses would be truthful. Yet, in fact, as we've clearly seen, Michael had become deeply suicidal. He was in so much pain, and in such an altered state of mind, that he had no conscious awareness to how dangerously suicidal he had become.

These are insights we need to understand if we are to support our warriors and first responders. They may tell us in all honesty, and with total confidence, that they are not in the suicidal mode when in fact they are in a dangerous place. A driving reason I took on this project was to use Michael's story to flush out these truths, truths that should change our collective understanding.

Suicide is the threat in the blind spot of many of our warriors and first responders. They are intensively trained to focus on the threat *outside of themselves* and socialized to act like invulnerable "heroes." As a result, it becomes very difficult for many of them to perceive how deeply dangerous the internal voice of despair can become. If someone had had the ability to discern his hidden pain, they would have seen that Michael didn't so much have a fear of death, as a fear of being cancelled out and then completely forgotten by his daughter.

Once Michael saw a seemingly "logical" path to ending his relentless pain, in a way that would cause him to be remembered and memorialized, his suicidality gripped him like an iron fist.

This is very common among the warriors and first responders that I have served. What masquerades as "heroism" is sometimes the manifestation of a death wish - a desire to flip the script of a death-by-cop suicide plan.

Regardless of how one is memorialized, the damage to loved ones can be all together permanent, profound, and long-lasting.

To speak directly to anyone who is in that dark place, I would say this: regardless of how strained these relationships may be, your loved ones want you to heal – not to die. The thought that your death is a gift to your loved ones is the fundamental lie that drives suicidal behavior. And it's a lie that is often only visible in retrospect, not when you are caught up in the suicidal mind state.

Michael has come through this valley. He is now meaningfully engaged in raising his daughter. He occasionally posts pictures - not obsessively, but in a normal way, of the adventures they have and the outings they take together. In these pictures, he is glowing with happiness and pride anytime he is in her presence. Michael is grateful to be there with her, raising her, as a steady loving presence in his daughter's life. He is finding healing, a little bit more every day. The voices of his demons have grown quiet, and the voice of hope has grown loud. Hope leads him on now.

So, before we go to the next chapter, it's important to remember this. Even when someone is dangerously suicidal, with the right insights and support, they can come through the valley and reconnect to hope, just as Michael did. But if people fail to understand the landscape of the mental warfare they face, this is much less likely to happen.

My deepest purpose is to help people see the battle with clarity and reveal the ways that the voice of despair tries to take us out. I've learned to look for different things, and ask different questions, based on new lines of understanding. This is what I teach, speak on, and write about. To learn more, please pick up a copy of my previous book, *WARRIOR: How to Support Those Who Protect Us,* or reach out if you'd like to have me give a talk for your group or organization.

10

WAKEUP CALL

This chapter includes some graphic content. It is necessary to tell the story of Michael's dear friend John Davison, a Vietnam Veteran and Walnut Creek reserve police officer whose suicide attempt pulled Michael out of his self-destructive tailspin. Thankfully, John is still with us, and this chapter is based on intimate interviews that I had with both John and Michael.

***

"On the night of the street fight, John and I were on patrol together. We got called out to a bar fight in downtown Walnut Creek. When we got there, we found 30 men brawling in the street in front of the bar. We were the only law enforcement presence on the scene, surrounded by 60 smashing fists. It was like being dropped into the middle of an alligator pond during a feeding frenzy.

So, John pulls out his baton and starts swinging it back and forth. Normally a soft-spoken, easy-going guy, John suddenly summoned a commanding presence that broke through their drunken minds. I was just as surprised as everyone else there. John ordered everyone to GET DOWN ON THE GROUND NOW! as he continued to swing his baton in a wide arc. Guys started dropping to the ground all around him, until all 30 of them were lying belly down in a circle around both of us. It was a glorious night."

— Michael Sugrue

(What follows is John's story, in his words)

When I got drafted to go to Vietnam, I had pictures in my mind of natives living in huts who would welcome us as rescuers. We'd fight for their freedom, stick it to the Commies, and come home as heroes.

It turned out that my year in Vietnam wasn't spent defending the Vietnamese people. I spent it instead defending myself against our own people, many of whom would have killed me if they had had a weapon.

After finishing my training, I was detailed to Long Binh Jail (LBJ) to serve as a prison guard in what was to be a temporary stockade for American soldiers. Some of the prisoners were a danger to their fellow soldiers when they arrived – others were suffering from PTSD and other mental health challenges.

They were brought in from the jungles of Vietnam, many of them with sores on their bodies, jungle rot on their feet and a thousand-yard stare. When the first ones arrived, I felt so bad for them. In the early days, I had the urge to be tearful when I saw these broken men, but I pushed that urge away until it went away for good.

Some of the prisoners were temporarily held at LBJ with a sentence considered "bad time." This meant that their time at the jail would not count towards their 365-day tour in Vietnam. Others were just passing through – on their way to places like Fort Leavenworth. We housed the minimum-security prisoners in tents and the maximum-security prisoners in sheet metal or wood boxes, or in CONEX containers. Imagine being locked up in a metal box with no windows in the wet, tropical heat of Vietnam.

We got shelled some nights – incoming mortars landing all around us. The ground rocked and I watched as the prisoners jumped from their beds to kneel and roll on the floor, weeping and praying for mercy. There was no way to escape it – we were all captives just the same. Somehow, their weeping and praying made me angry. We were all just sitting ducks – what was the point of crying about it?

LBJ was greatly understaffed. It would take about 300 guards to adequately control the situation, and to keep ourselves and the prisoners safe from each other. There were less than 100 guards. Racial tension was very high between some of the African American prisoners and the guards, especially the white guards. They frequently told us that they would kill us if given any chance.

Under continual threat like this, some of the guards had lost connection with their humanity. One of the tactics I saw some guards use to subdue the most dangerous prisoners was to place a wooden 2x4 on the back of their heads and hit it repeatedly with a hammer. It didn't crack their skulls, but it scrambled their brains.

One night, I heard a terrible sound coming from inside of a CONEX container. Another guard explained "prisoner breakdown" as he ran by. I grasped the wire fence with my fingers and watched the rocking of the CONEX container as someone inside flung himself wildly against the wall. I began to shake as I gripped the fence so tightly that blood started oozing from my fingers. I broke down, my body shaking with tears and a terrible grasping despair. After running back to my quarters, I stripped down and stood in the shower for a very long time, trying to wash all the badness away. But it didn't erase the horrors inside my head.

I was there for the 1968 riot, when about 200 inmates attacked and attempted to overthrow the guards. They set fire to the buildings, burning the mess hall, the barber shop, the latrine and some of the administration and finance building. Black and white rioters attacked each other in brutal, racially driven ways. The prisoners barricaded themselves inside the administration building for over a week. The riot left more than 50 inmates and 63 guards injured. A prisoner was beaten to death with steel rods.

I survived that year of captivity and continual threat from American inmates by the skin of my teeth.

***

Being a prison guard is about the last thing I ever imagined doing. By nature, I'm easy going. While I was in military training in Augusta, GA, one of my favorite memories was strolling into the room with my guitar and singing "This little light of mine…I'm gonna let it shine" to perk up the spirits of my brothers in arms.

They began to smile and joined in. My heart was pounding as we went from song to song. It was the first time I had felt truly happy since leaving my home. I was doing what I did best, making others laugh and sweeping everyone along with my music, to help them forget the misery of that time. This memory shows who I am at the core.

I had a good childhood, with parents who loved me. To give you a window into some of my childhood, you need to understand the relationship I had with my dad. He was a successful salesman who took a personal interest in helping me learn the trade. He helped me develop a sales pitch for things I would sell door to door to the women in our affluent town. As a very young kid, I would knock on the door and say 'good morning, ma'am. I've got something that every woman in Orinda needs…(long pause) greeting cards." They would burst out laughing but I didn't get the joke until much later. My dad also had me selling Christmas wreaths door to door, but we came to find out that what we were selling by accident was actually funeral wreaths. My dad made me give him 30% of everything I earned. I got to keep the other 70%. When I was older, he gave me access to an account he had set aside where all my earnings went. That account helped me pay for college. That was the kind of family support I had.

When I came home from Vietnam in 1969, I was on a natural high for the first few weeks. After a few months of this, though, it all crashed down. I suddenly had an overwhelming feeling of depression, a feeling like some ghastly creature was gripping me. All the sadness I pushed down, the tears I suppressed when American soldiers came to LBJ, being surrounded by broken men in despair, my own captivity, the constant fear and threat to our lives, having to treat our own soldiers like my enemies (because they would have killed me if they had the chance), it all collapsed in on me. I had continual nightmares of being trapped. I lost my job and spent my days in my mom's basement, exhausted, and spinning out of control. All the sorrow and the badness felt like a virus that had been sitting there waiting to take control of me.

My sister's support became critical to me during this time in my life. Joanne was always on my side. She was one of the most important people in bringing me home after I returned from Vietnam. My mom stepped up as well and helped me get counseling. Their support and the counseling arrested the tailspin I was in. I stabilized and reconnected to the idea of having a future worth living for.

Ten years after I went to Vietnam, in 1978, I took a job as a reserve police officer for the city of Walnut Creek. It was a position I would hold for 35 years, from 1978 to 2014.

A reserve officer rides out on patrols with the full-time officers. It's an important job because we are their eyes and ears. We are the ones who have their back when they make a traffic stop or go into other potentially dangerous situations.

All the reserve officers wanted to ride out with Michael Sugrue. In fact, we fought among ourselves to ride with him. He drove that car like NASCAR legend Parnelli Jones. He was just plain good – no one ever got away from Michael. When we had to make a traffic stop or go into a situation, he got dead serious. He was a total professional. Between things, we'd spent hours talking, joking about some of our past dates with women and other things. I told him about my time in Vietnam, and he gave me dating advice. He told me that I needed to go online to meet women, and I told him, "Michael, I don't even have a computer." I could talk to him about anything. Over countless nights together in the patrol car, we became very close friends –family, really, to each other.

We worked late at night, often on the graveyard shift. Sometimes I would doze off. Some of the officers would jerk the car to the right really hard so that you'd hit your head on the door and wake up, but Michael never did that. He was always kind. But there was this one

time when he pulled into a Starbucks before our shift. He turned
and said, "OK, John, I don't want you falling asleep on me tonight"
and he buys me this drink that had something like ginseng in it. I
stayed awake for 72 hours straight. [When Michael and John and I
talked about this night, Michael cracked a smile and said, "I did you
a favor really. Think of all the things you got done those three days.
You got your car washed, and your lawn mowed at 3 a.m....]

***

I was especially close with Michael, but I was close to other officers
as well – that happens when you risk your life together repeatedly.
Some people bond when they go through something difficult just
once. This kind of bonding happens over and over when people
ride out on patrols together. I remember this one time when I was
with another officer. We got called out to pick up a guy who was
high on PCP. He was out of his mind. He had grabbed a civil war
sword and had sliced himself and his girlfriend up badly. She was
still alive but there was blood everywhere. The PCP gave him
superhuman strength. It took two of us – me and the other officer
- to push him forcefully into the back of the patrol car after we
arrested him. I remember touching his forearm. Though it was
slippery with blood, it felt like it was made of concrete. The PCP
had turned him into something like the Incredible Hulk.

As we were driving him to the Martinez jail, he started spitting on the back of my neck through the wire barrier between the front seats and the back of the patrol car. He asked me "were you in 'Nam?" and when I said yes, he said something like, "It's going down now…" I asked my fellow officer for permission to subdue him with a can of mace and he said, "Yes, please do." What I didn't realize was that the windows were locked so I maced all of us. There we were, all of us choking and coughing, totally disoriented, our eyes streaming with tears. When we finally arrived at the Martinez jail, all of us looking like something the dog dragged in, they said that the prisoner was too injured to be received at the jail. They told us to take him to the county hospital to get his wounds treated first.

When we got to the county hospital, he was put on a gurney, still completely out of his mind. As we helped transfer him to the gurney, he sunk his teeth into my partner's arm. My partner used his baton to knock him back flat against the gurney. We heard the shrill voice of a doctor from across the room saying "police brutality" without understanding that my partner was effectively defending himself against a man who had turned into something like a rabid dog. The doctor walked up to the prisoner, now secured on the gurney, and he spit right in her face. Her face hardened and she said, "get this son of a bitch out of here." People make all kinds of judgments about what we do in law enforcement when they are at a safe distance. They often see a different side of the story when they are in the same situations as we are.

We later heard that when he came off his PCP high, he wanted to know the names of the officers who brought him in (me and my partner). He said, "I can't remember their names now, but they were cool. I really liked those guys."

Anyway, I had many good years with the officers, to include Michael most of all. I was in a relationship with a beautiful lady, and I had a nice home. I had fleeting thoughts of sorrow and grief about Vietnam, but it never really overran me until 2016. In 2016, I lost my two dogs, one right after the other. They were extremely bonded to each other. I think the second one died of a broken heart. Those two losses brought Vietnam flooding back to me – the sorrow and the despair. When I was off duty, I spent full days sitting in my room, overwhelmed by hopeless thoughts.

The theme in my thoughts during that time was that with my dogs gone, I had nothing to look forward to in life. I withdrew because I was ashamed of what I felt. I was ashamed about the suicidal thoughts and the feeling that I had lost control of my life. I was ashamed that I was falling apart and didn't want everyone to see how bad it had gotten. So, I retreated and hid myself away while I formed a plan to end my life.

Then one day, I decided to do it. As chance would have it, Michael was one of the two officers to get the call about the suicide attempt. He showed up as soon as I had been transported to the local ER. They rolled me in on a gurney, covered in blood. I distinctly remember Michael looking deep into my eyes with his piercing gaze and saying, "John, you're going to make it." He was willing me to live.

I had been through a year of Hell in Vietnam. But the hardest thing I ever had to do was to tell the people I care about that I was suicidal. I was so afraid that I would lose everyone who loved and respected me. What actually happened is that nobody in my life ever said a critical word to me about my suicide attempt. Again, my sister Joanne stepped up in support of me, taking me into her home during my recovery, while I was in an outpatient program at a hospital in Monterey. Her family's kindness and support of me was remarkable. In addition, my sister's friend Maurine went above and beyond to support me during this time of need. She proved to be one of the truest friends that I have ever known. Also, as I was recovering from my suicide attempt, my fellow officers would sit with me – overnight even – continually talking with me until I was well again. They had my back, just like I had had theirs, all those years while we were on patrol together.

And when I got to a place of recovery from my darkest period, Michael was quick to tell me this: "John, you saved my life. I realized that I needed help based on what you did."

Doc Springer's Reflections

The preceding chapter was based mainly on an intimate conversation with John while we sat together on my back porch. The sun was shining, and the flowers were waving in the breeze as he walked me through his battle with darkness. At the end of our conversation, we put Michael on speaker phone. Michael teased John with his reaction to the "3 days awake" incident.

But Michael also said this, "John, when you were in a tailspin, we knew that you were struggling. We were reaching out to you because of it. Some of the guys and I were calling you and going out to lunch with you to check up on you. But maybe we weren't pressing as hard as we should have."

When people are struggling, it takes a rare form of relational courage on both sides to bring them back from the brink. Michael and his brothers were doing their best to show up for John in his time of need.

When people have altered, and our gut tells us that they are not OK, we must summon our courage to be a kind of "sapper" in their lives. A "Sapper" in the Marine Corps is someone who clears mines for other Marines (among other things). In other words, a "Sapper" blows up the things that would kill his brothers and sisters in arms to give them a clear path through dangerous terrain.

In terms of preventing suicide, we can be a "sapper" for someone when we blow up the obstacles that block them from sharing their hidden pain. In the context of these conversations, we can be a "sapper" by:

1. Emphasizing the universality of human suffering and the commonality of suicidal thoughts
2. Blowing up shame and smashing stigma by leveling with them about our own mental battles

The fact that this may not have happened is no judgment on Michael or his fellow officers, who were doing the best they knew to help John at that time. The situation Michael describes is all too common. One person is silently struggling, unable to overcome their shame and acknowledge it, and the other doesn't have psychological x-ray vision into how dire the danger has become. This is why we must understand that "recognizing the signs of distress" and asking bold questions like, "Have you been thinking about hurting or killing yourself" is not sufficient if we want to keep our loved ones in the fight.

In fact, when we ask this question of someone who is struggling, if we do not lay the groundwork by expressing vulnerability first ourselves, we heighten the chance that they will simply continue to deny their struggles. Having denied their struggles once makes it all the harder for them to reverse direction and acknowledge these struggles.

<u>This is a critical point</u>.

We often stay in the channel that we build for ourselves. Like Peter who told Jesus that he would never deny their relationship, then promptly denied it not just once, but 2 more times, the pull to be consistent in our human communications is very strong. If you ask "the suicide risk assessment question" in the wrong context, you might get a less-than-candid response that moves the other person further from the reach of truth telling.

If you are a peer, not a professional therapist, and you think that all you have to do is "ask the question" about *their* suicidal state, without first acknowledging that you have had times of mental battles or other struggles yourself, you might drive them further into isolation and shame. Because asking this question without first leveling the power in the relationship does not create space for courageous honesty.

To be clear, I'm not saying that you must have been suicidal yourself at one time to help someone who is suicidal. It may be as easy as saying something like,

"I'm noticing a change in you that reminds me of times when I've had some serious mental battles. Mental battles – even really serious ones – are part of life for all of us. I know because I've been there myself. You are really important to me and there is nothing you could say that would change how I view you – nothing. I feel anxious because I see that something has shifted in you lately. I want to make sure you know you can tell me anything. What I don't want is to risk losing someone I love as much as you. Because of how important you are to me, I need to ask you, 'have you been thinking about hurting or killing yourself?'"

For too long, the field of suicide prevention has been focused on only one side of the equation, as if "recognize the signs and ask the hard question" is enough to save lives. To be sure, this will save some lives, but the more important thing is to create and maintain a "culture of emotional courage" within our relationships. And we do this by walking point, expressing our own struggles often enough that it becomes normal – not shameful – to be a human who struggles – sometimes mightily – at times. This practice builds the deep trust we must draw on to keep ourselves and those we love in the fight.

This is critical because without this kind of trust, lethal secrets stay secret. When these secrets get exposed in the context of a relationship of deep trust, they lose their power. This is why I continue to repeat, as a theme, this fundamental point: *When we connect, we survive.*

11

THE BEGINNING OF HOPE

From the previous chapter, we learned that John's suicide attempt disrupted Michael's self-destructive course. But how did it do this exactly? In this chapter, listen for the critical moment, the turning point, that moved Michael to ask for help. This moment shows us what has a power that is greater than despair.

***

When the 911 call about an attempted suicide came to the police department, I was sitting with a fellow sergeant. He turned to me and said, "Hey that's John's address!"

My gut twisted into a knot, and I started running to my patrol car. I knew that John would be taken to a certain local hospital, so I moved fast to get there in time. We arrived at the same exact moment. As John relays, I stood over him on the gurney, looking deep into his eyes, and willing him to live.

John was taken straight into surgery. My fellow officers and I waited in a separate part of the hospital along with John's sister. We shared memories of John to stave off the feeling of dread that we might lose him. Late that night, after hours of waiting, we were informed that he had been stabilized. He was in terrible condition, but he was going to survive.

After he was released from the emergency room, John was transferred to a locked unit where he was monitored very closely for the next 72 hours. In my career as a police sergeant, I had done lots of "5150s" – in other words, placing people on involuntary holds for being a danger to themselves. However, I had never seen the inside of a facility where people are taken after they are put on a 5150. In my mind, what I was picturing was a scene in the movie "One Flew Over the Cuckoo's Nest."

Shortly after his transfer there, I showed up at the locked treatment facility to visit John. As I walked through the hall, there were people who looked dazed - some with walkers, and others staring at the ground and shuffling by. John was lying on a twin sized hospital bed at the end of the hall, in a single occupancy room. There was nothing in the room but the bed he was lying on. He looked pale and weak. He was not his usual upbeat self, but a shell of the man he usually is – obviously medicated. Clearly, his recovery was going to be a long road. My stomach tightened into a familiar knot as I had thoughts like, "How did I miss this? And now that he's attempted to end his life once, how are we going to stop him from doing it again?"

In that moment, looking at John in his weakened state, I finally connected with the thought that I had been trying the same thing myself. This immediately brought on an overwhelming feeling of guilt. It made me realize that if I did die by my own hand, the people I love most in the world would start to take blame onto themselves - just like I was doing with John's suicide attempt. This incredibly painful realization prepared and motivated me to seek help no matter what it cost me.

The holidays arrived shortly after John's near-fatal suicide attempt. Since the fatal shooting happened at Christmas time, this time of year has always been really hard for me. The pressure began to build steadily over the month of December. Whenever possible, I tried to arrange circumstances to help me get through this painful time. Being around people was a very important part of this plan.

In this particular year, the divorce and custody proceedings were ongoing with my soon-to-be-ex-wife. My daughter was staying with her mother. I found myself totally alone during the anniversary of my trauma.

For many years, exercise has been my stress relief. I headed to the gym because I've long associated working out with feeling better – beating back the demons of depression and the daily trauma of my work. As a first responder, I've also felt intense pressure for many years to put on an image, to mask my pain. When I put my uniform on, I was continually aware that I was representing not only myself, but everyone else in my profession. For years, I had told myself that as long as I get to the gym, and continue to look sharp, I would be OK.

On this day, these defenses crumbled. I couldn't stop thinking about how much my life had changed since the night of the shooting. I had lost my identity as a police officer. Instead of feeling pride, I felt embarrassment and shame. I knew that I was living a lie – projecting an image of strength at work, while I was privately self-destructing. I had lost my marriage and was in the middle of a custody battle for my daughter. All I had left was my daughter and my life. My daughter was the person I was afraid to lose more than life itself.

I left the gym, went out to my car, and broke down. I sat in my car alone for over 2 hours, experiencing something between a flashback and a nightmare of the future. The mental movie that I kept playing out in my mind was based on having served in the honor guard in the past. The honor guard attends military funerals to ensure that service members are afforded the honors they've earned when they pass away. My mind brought back a memory of a particular funeral where a little girl ran to her father's casket. Weeping with broken-hearted tears, she wrapped her arms around the casket, trying to hold her father one last time. Into that mental movie, my mind inserted this set of images:

I see my ex-wife walking my daughter towards a casket. My daughter is wearing a knee length formal dress with a bow in her hair. She lets go of her mother's hand and runs the last 15 feet to the casket. She wraps her arms around the top of the casket, attempting to hug it, and cries out "Daddy" as she breaks down sobbing. She's six years old. I'm in the casket.

In that moment, with total clarity, I resolved that I couldn't do this to my daughter – I couldn't continue down the path towards suicide.

In comparison to causing this kind of pain for my daughter, I didn't care about my career, or position as a sergeant – I just knew I needed to make a total commitment to healing my trauma. It was during that painful breakdown, sitting in my car alone outside the gym, that I called the on-duty watch commander.

The watch commander, for those unfamiliar, is the person you call if you're sick and unable to come to work. Thankfully, my friend Andy Brown happened to be on duty that day. But this was not a casual conversation with a friend, testing the waters to see how he'd respond when I told him I was suffering. In law enforcement, when you inform the watch commander about a physical or mental health challenge, you are going on the record, and you can't take it back.

When he picked up the phone, I said, "Andy, I need help. I can't do this anymore. I need to take time off work to get better." Even though we were friends, I didn't tell him that I was suicidal. That was too scary. What I did say is that I had been suffering in silence since the shooting and that I needed to go see someone to get some help. He recommended that I reach out to an LCSW that works with our department. She's a good person, but there's always this question that comes up about whether you can truly open up to anybody who is associated with the department - anyone who is paid by the department. From my years of working on the police force and talking to my fellow officers, I know that this is a common concern and a major reason why people do not get help when they need it.

Given the holidays, she wasn't able to see me in person right away but was willing to speak with me by phone and assess the situation.

Based on that call, she signed me out for a few more days of work leave. She also relayed that based on department policy, I would need to see the workman's compensation doctor through Occupational Medicine ("OCMED") if I needed additional time off work.

For the next several days, that evaluation was all I could think of.

What would the OCMED provider ask me?

How much would I need to share?

Would I break down again in front of a stranger?

Would they believe me even though my struggle is not physically verifiable?

A few days later I went to my appointment. OCMED is staffed by general practitioners who work for the city. They have the power to write an employee off from work or direct them to return to work. Since I had sent several people to OCMED in my role as a supervisor, I knew that most cases were referred due to back or knee pain. The most common outcome was that the officer was given some motrin, told to ice the affected area and return to work the following day. Taking people off work is expensive, while getting them efficiently back to work is expedient for the city, who pays the salaries for the OCMED providers.

OCMED operates out of a big commercial office building about two blocks from the police department – not a comfortable place for me to be. When you walk in the front door, there is a row of metal chairs with cloth bottoms and backs sitting five in a row in a common waiting area. In other words, no privacy. As soon as I walked through the door, I started to battle an inner voice that whispered, "Should I really even be here? What if someone asks me why I'm here? Should I just go back to work and tell them I'm feeling much better?"

As I sat in the waiting area, I was worried about seeing someone that I know, which would raise questions about why I was there. I arrived at 8 a.m. as instructed and waited to be seen. All day long, I waited, feeling exposed, for 7 hours, between 8 a.m. and 3 p.m., at which point I was finally called in to see the doctor.

I had a bad gut feeling based on the way he carried himself and the condescending way he spoke to me. There was no sign of compassion in this provider. Despite this, I recounted the shooting, the lawsuit, and how my life was falling apart. I unzipped myself. I shared all of it, hoping that he would hear me.

In response, he said to me, "you're a cop though. This is what you do. The best thing for you to do is go back to work."

I was speechless for a moment. Then I got really angry. I said to him, "Hold on, you've got to be kidding me. You're telling me that you want me to go back to work knowing that I have a fully loaded weapon?"

And he said, "Yes that's what I'm saying."

He then told me that he himself had grown up in a rough neighborhood and had witnessed one of his friends get shot, but that he had gone on with his life regardless. He shared this story in a totally cold, clinical way – using it as a throw-down example to shame me for being impacted by the traumas I shared with him.

At this point in the interaction, to be totally honest, I wanted to punch him in the face. I said, "This is unbelievable! Is there anyone else I can talk to?"

I had broken open my soul to a doctor I'd never met because he had the power to help me at my lowest point. In response, he denied my pain and essentially told me to 'suck it up.'

I stormed out of his office, straight into rush-hour traffic all the way home. My blood pressure was up. My face was hot. I felt sick to my stomach, humiliated and really angry. On the ride home, I called the same social worker who is attached to our department. I expressed my frustration and outrage over the way he had responded to everything I shared with him. I'm grateful to say that she took action quickly and called the Captain, telling him that I needed to be off work until she would be able to see me a few days later.

When I saw her, I didn't tell her that I was suicidal. I told her everything else - that I was depressed and anxious and that I was drinking too much. Always, in the back of my mind, there was a fear that because she works for the department, I might lose my job if I were to tell her that I was suicidal. I did not want to end up on a

5150, locked away like John had been, with my gun taken away, and my career over.

She referred me to an outside social worker who only works with first responders. This program was covered under our City's Worker's Compensation Program.

A couple days later, I arrived for my first appointment with my assigned counselor. I was greeted by a tall lady with a friendly face in her mid-60s who looked like she was from Viking stock. I sat down with her and immediately told her that I needed a therapist who understands police officers and first responders. She told me a story from her background that immediately made me feel comfortable.

In total contrast to the OCMED provider, when she looked at me, I could feel her warmth and compassion. She had a way of smiling that communicated to me: 'I see your pain. I get it.' When she shared the story from her past, she showed me how it had impacted her, and as a result, this deepened my sense that she could understand my pain.

That day in her office marked the beginning of hope for me. I was able to open myself to somebody who is truly safe and who 'gets it.' It was the opposite of the experience I had had with the worker's compensation evaluator. Therapy unfolded over the next several months - two sessions per week. She continued to earn my trust. I began to heal.

A few months into treatment, she mentioned her affiliation with a program called the West Coast Post Trauma Retreat. The West Coast Post Trauma Retreat is a highly sought-after treatment program that is geared towards police officers and first responders. I had wanted to attend for a long time but had never had the courage to ask to go to the program. With her support, I was able to apply and be accepted into the program.

In addition I began to attend first responder, peer-support meetings. These are 60-minute meetings set up like 12 step groups, but with greater flexibility. Substance abuse and addiction are not a requirement for being part of this. As I soon learned, some of the people in the group identified themselves as simply "JFU" ("just fucked up").

The key is that these circles are for people in the first responder communities, to share with each other in a truly confidential way. To enter the group, you first speak with a point of contact, who pre-screens everyone who wants to attend these groups. In this way, it's a protected and safe space for first responders.

As I sat in the circle with fellow first responders, I was told that there is no pressure to participate. I could just listen and take it all in. I sat and listened for the first three sessions. It was incredible to me that people I didn't know were sharing about their deepest pain, giving me their phone number, and encouraging me without knowing me at all.

I kept waiting for the other shoe to drop but it never did. People in the group opened up about a lot of things that people don't usually talk about. Several members of the group expressed shame about getting hooked on opiates after sustaining injuries on the job. Others talked about their addiction to alcohol or a pattern of being unfaithful in their marriages. They spoke about their deepest traumas – fatal car accidents and witnessing the deaths of children. As first responders, we are supposed to save those most vulnerable – so the deaths of children leave us feeling helpless. Some of us feel like failures when we cannot save a child.

The first time I shared, I looked around the room to see if people were acting different or looking at me like I was crazy. Nothing but positive responses. A whole new world opened up to me - people supporting each other without any personal agenda or ego. This is what Doc Springer calls the "power of Tribe," and, as she says, it has a power that is greater than despair. As I stayed connected to these circles, I continued to heal and felt my hope growing every day.

I think if I had had this kind of support after the night of the shooting – that is, a trusted therapist, and circles where I could safely talk about my trauma, I would still be working. The confidential first responder support groups are the first resource I tell people about nowadays. First responders who suffer from trauma need peers who get it and who don't judge each other. They need places to heal without fear of anything bad coming from sharing their stories. In a circle of peers, we can ride through the ups and downs together. Our work as first responders is challenging. It's not a rainbow path. We all know the realities of the job, and we extend each other respect and compassion. I went to those meetings for over two and a half years. It was a really big part of my recovery.

Doc Springer's Reflections

Before I worked with those in military or first responder roles, I treated a private practice sample of highly educated, well paid civilian patients. They loved coming to therapy. It was an opportunity to quiet the noise in their lives. Therapy gave them a chance to reflect on their current patterns and develop continual goals for their own growth. Therapy was a luxury and a status symbol for many of my patients ("I have an expensive house, an expensive car, and an expensive therapist").

I also taught personal growth at the University of Florida, as part of my doctoral program. I had a class of about 100 undergraduates who were keenly interested in learning about themselves. Personal growth was my signature course, the one for which I was nominated for a teaching award. It was a course that pushed them to actively form their core identity based on their deeper values, something many people never do across the arc of their lives. My students were fascinated by the case stories I shared from my practicum work as a therapist-in-training. Many of them openly talked about their own therapy experiences, in class-wide discussions, all 100 of us.

When I started working with veterans, and first responders, everything changed. As I wrote about in my previous book *WARRIOR,*

- Many of my patients did not come to therapy by their own choosing. They were strongly encouraged – sometimes by loved ones, and sometimes by a legal authority – to come to therapy.
- Many of my patients didn't care about the Ph.D. on my wall. In fact, some felt that it only increased the gap in our life experiences. While I was teaching undergraduates, running a research lab, or locked away writing my dissertation, they had been putting their lives on the line.
- In short, in our initial sessions, this group of patients was looking for a reason to never return to therapy.

There are many reasons for this.

Some of it has to do with a hidden class system in the practice of healthcare that creates a deeper culture, and trust deficit, between civilian mental health providers, and those in first responder roles. I wrote about this extensively in my book WARRIOR. I talked about how the very things we are taught to do in graduate school – to display our diplomas, direct the intake assessment process, and form a treatment plan based on our expertise, may actually increase the trust gap with some patients. I talked about how the higher order calling of a healer is to build the trust that allows our patients to share their hidden pain. I talked about how trust outranks rank.

There is also a fear on the part of patients that therapy isn't safe – that what they share may jeopardize their careers and their livelihood. When trust is broken by systems, or individual practitioners, it makes the work of building trust so much more difficult with everyone in that group of patients. Word of any breach of trust by a mental health provider spreads like wildfire. (*"Did you hear what happened to Shari? She went to the psychologist provided by the Employee Assistance Program (EAP) and he made a diagnosis that caused her to be put on restricted duty"*).

First responders learn to trust people, not systems. They may come to trust an individual "Doc" to hear their hidden pain, but initially, there is often a deep trust gap that must be overcome. A new provider, who is unknown to a given first responder, typically has a lot to prove before trust is earned. As I wrote about in WARRIOR, when a warrior or first responder breaks through a wall of internal resistance and asks for help, the stakes are very high, and the window of opportunity for building trust is very narrow.

Some providers, like the OCMED physician, deepen the trust gap, and confirm everything the first responder feared when he or she asked for help. Their concerns may be minimized or overlooked by these providers. Others, like the therapist Michael saw after the OCMED appointment, prove that they are "safe" and that they "get it."

While interactions with therapists are a factor in getting the help that is needed, this is not the only potential obstacle to care. On the side of the patient, another potential barrier to treatment is what Michael describes repeatedly– the belief that strength is projecting an image that one is not affected by things that would impact most people.

In warrior and first responder culture, the definition of "strength" that is upheld is very different from the way that strength is viewed in therapy. Among first responders, strength is defined as perseverance in the face of physical, mental, and emotional pain. This kind of strength is not only valued, but it is expected and required.

For example, like military service members, police officers

frequently tell each other to "suck it up." They believe that their minds are strong enough to conquer pain, physical and emotional, by compartmentalizing and essentially ignoring pain. They are taught that being strong means dealing with things by themselves, and that asking for help makes them weak.

I'd like to suggest that this kind of thinking needs a different set of insights.

From my perspective, pretending a problem doesn't exist is often easier than confronting it. Being humble enough to admit a problem requires strength of character. Successfully addressing a problem requires the internal will to adapt and overcome, and to persist in the face of obstacles.

As a quick thought exercise, ask yourself, of the two paths laid out below, which one is the harder path?

Which is the Harder Path?

Keeping your mask on	Admitting personal struggles
Pretending you don't need help	Asking for help
Trying to handle it on your own	Seeking mental health treatment
Dropping out of treatment in anger/disgust	Being persistent until you link up with a good 'Doc'

Changing habits and patterns is hard for all of us, and it can be physically and emotionally painful. A healer does his or her best to help alleviate emotional pain during the process of treatment. But sometimes, personal growth requires us to confront painful experiences directly. In some cases, the best way to deal with obstacles is to charge straight through them.

We may have to break down before we can become stronger, just as muscles get stronger after muscle fibers are torn. At other times, we need to learn to live good lives, while in pain. Viewed in this light, it becomes easy to see how avoiding behavioral health issues is the easier, more comfortable path, while getting help takes courage.

12

A CAREER-ENDING BETRAYAL

To be under attack from people outside of our closest circle is very challenging. But to be betrayed by those within our circle is even more devastating. In this chapter, Michael describes the string of interactions that led him to retire from law enforcement.

**

My connection with a trusted counselor, attendance of the West Coast Post Trauma Retreat and regular meetings with safe people, in confidential peer support circles, was repairing a trust that had been so badly damaged by years of trauma. I had been off duty on official injury status for several months. On a monthly basis, I was required to have a psychologist sign off on whether I needed to stay off duty or return to work.

As part of the West Coast Post Trauma Retreat, I was given a mentor, somewhat like an AA sponsor, but with a focus on recovery coaching. My sponsor helped me set several specific goals that were part of my recovery plan. One of my goals was to disrupt the pattern of obsessively taking selfies with my daughter during our time together. He urged me to spend more quality time with her - making positive memories that would get me living again, instead of worrying about whether I might die by my own hand or otherwise.

Ever since my daughter was very young, one of the big traditions in our family had been to take an annual trip to Disneyland. Our first trip was when she was two years old. Every year, around July 4, it was a big event that we all looked forward to. It was symbolic to us - a celebration of how we were so blessed to have her in our lives. Every year we stayed at the same hotel as part of this family tradition. We had never missed a year until our marriage dissolved.

While we were going through a divorce, and I was simultaneously defending myself in the legal battle related to the shooting, my wife took my daughter to Disneyland without me. It was a huge blow. I felt really left out. It was a painful reminder that I was missing out on a critical time in my daughter's life.

So, when my sponsor asked me to think about how I would like to make memories for my daughter, taking her to Disneyland was the first thing that came to mind. I decided to surprise her on Father's Day weekend. I posted on my Facebook account that I was looking forward to celebrating Father's Day in Disneyland with my daughter.

When I picked her up from school and told her that we were going to LA for the weekend, her face lit up with a huge smile that I'll never forget. She was six years old. We went back to my place and collected her things for the weekend. She filled up the entire backseat with books and stuffed animals for the long drive to Southern California. The mood was jovial. As I peeked into the rearview mirror, we made eye contact and she had a huge smile on her face. She sat in the backseat in her booster chair, wearing a pink and orange dress and her custom-made Mickey Mouse ears.

On the way down, the phone rang. When I saw the main number of the police department, I got immediate anxiety. I let it go to voicemail. The message was from a lady in HR. Her tone was friendly and casual with no urgency at all. She said she was checking in on me and that I could give her a call back whenever convenient.

Here is the exact transcript of what the message said, and it was delivered in a very casual, friendly tone:

"Hey Mike, it's [name of caller] with Human Resources at the City. I'm actually here with Capt. [name]. And we were just callin' to check in with you. It's been awhile since we talked. I've...I'm obviously, I'm in the loop on your work status. But we just kinda [sic] wanted to check in with you. I know you attended the retreat. Wanted to see how things are going and sorta [sic] get an updated status directly from you. So, if you wouldn't mind giving me a call back. If you happen to get this message, if you could let me know when would be a good time for us to give you a call so we can all chat together, I would really appreciate it. It's a little before 4 on Thursday and my direct line is (gives number). Thank you."

I decided to return the call on Monday. I really wanted to focus on my daughter. However, my stomach started churning and I began to feel acute anxiety about the call.

As soon as we got to the hotel - the same one we always went to – we took our bags to our room and changed into our swimsuits. We went down to the pool and hot tub. It was the perfect way to start what I had hoped would be a perfect weekend. I did take a few pictures of my daughter with that same huge smile on her face swimming in the pool or relaxing in the hot tub. But I didn't have the same underlying motivation to preserve this memory so that my daughter would know I loved her if I wasn't around someday. I didn't have the same obsessive need to take selfie after selfie of the two of us. My anxiety began to dissolve, and I began to enjoy every moment with her.

The next morning, we headed across the street to breakfast - the same place we always eat on the first morning during our annual trip to Disneyland. It was a restaurant that caters to Disneyland tourists. My daughter ordered the same thing she always did - pancakes shaped like Mickey Mouse's head.

As we were enjoying our breakfast together and looking forward to the day ahead with great anticipation, the phone rang again. It was my Captain from the Walnut Creek Police Department. He insisted that we needed to speak right away. Here's the transcription of that message which I've also kept as a record ever since:

"Hey Mike, [Captain's name] down at the PD. Just left a message on your cell phone. [HR person] and I tried to call you yesterday and left

a message as well. It's about 11:15. Please give me a call back ASAP

(leaves number). If I don't hear from ya [sic] today (Friday) I'm going

to need you to come down 0800 on Monday morning at the PD –

0800 - 0900 sometime between 08 and 09 so please give me a call

today. And if for some reason you don't get this sometime over the

weekend, if not, I need to see you on Monday morning. Technically,

you're supposed to be available all through the week and I don't think

we have any vacation time scheduled for ya [sic] so I'm assuming you

are in town, so please give me a call. Thanks Bye."

We left breakfast early and we immediately returned to our hotel room. I called him back and we had a lengthy conversation while my daughter was in the room – not what I wanted, but I had no other choice. Never once did he say that he knew I was out of town or at Disneyland although later this became clear. In retrospect, I can see that someone I work with had mentioned it based on my Facebook post. With my daughter right there in the same room, he told me that it was "taking quite awhile" for me to get better. He asked me whether I had ever thought about retiring from the police force and he told me that if I agreed to retire, he would make it painless. After the call, I was so angry that I wanted to drive straight home. But I didn't. I stayed the course and took my daughter to Disneyland. I was sick to my stomach with stress all day, trying not to show her how distracted and upset I felt.

Four days later, on June 17, I received an official letter via certified mail from Walnut Creek Police Department signed by the same Captain. Here is what it said (transcribed exactly):

"Hi Mike,

I understand you may have been on vacation recently to Disneyland. If that is the case, you will need to put in for time off. I'm happy to help if you want to tell me how many hours and which leave bank to use. Your current totals are below. Are there any other vacations you have taken since being off that you need to report? If so, please call me or Lt (name) and we will assist you with this reporting.

For clarification, while on leave you still need to be available to some extent (return calls within a reasonable amount of time, etc.) and any time for vacation or travel must be covered by your leave or comp time. Let me know if you have any questions."

(Leave balances shown)

(Signed by the Captain and the HR person who had called the previous week)

These rules had never been made clear to me. No one had told me that I had to remain within close distance to the Walnut Creek Police Department while I was on injury leave. I wasn't on call. I wasn't even on light duty. I had made no attempt to hide the fact that I was going to Disneyland with my daughter over Father's Day – I had even posted it on Facebook, which is how he must have learned that I was in Southern California.

None of this ever came up in his previous Friday morning voicemail message (in fact, just the opposite – he made a point to say "I assume you are in town" in his voicemail). None of this came up during our lengthy call on Friday morning when I called him back immediately from our hotel room. The letter showed that he was obviously aware that I was out of town, and the fact that he didn't mention this in either of these interactions made me feel that he was trying to trap me.

Immediately my gut twisted into a knot, and I wondered if I was going to be fired. I felt like I had been betrayed by the very people who are supposed to be my family. Getting this letter in the mail, after the two previous messages from this Captain pushed me to the decision to retire. I couldn't imagine going back to work with people that I didn't trust. How could I even walk into that building again, let alone risk my life next to people that had stabbed me in the back like this?

My driving thought at the time was, "OK, I'm done with this –
I'm OUT."

In early August, I initiated paperwork to start the formal
retirement process.

There's a law in California that you can't retire if there are any open
or ongoing investigations against you. This law was put into place
because people were retiring instead of being investigated and held
accountable for wrongdoings. If you are convicted of wrongdoing,
you can be fired immediately and will lose your entire retirement.
Everyone knew about the change in the law but there should be no
way it would affect me. I didn't have any charges against me, or
ongoing investigations when I filed my retirement. My record was
clean and clear.

A few weeks later, out of nowhere, that changed. An officer I had
not worked with in over a year made a sudden allegation that I had
pressured him to change something in one of his reports. Based on
this, I received this letter (shared just as written):

TO: Sergeant Michael Sugrue

FROM: CAPT (WCPD)

RE: Administrative Investigation

9/5/2017

The Police Department is conducting an administrative investigation into alleged misconduct by you. Lieutenant [name] has been assigned to investigate this matter. This notification is intended to make sure you are aware of your rights and obligations during the investigation process.

You will be contacted by Lieutenant [name] to set a date and time for your interview. Prior to your interview, you are ordered not to discuss this incident with anyone other than those authorized by me, and/or those authorized by law. If you require clarification with whom you may speak, contact me immediately.

We want to do as much as possible to accommodate your current leave status. We are sensitive to how an administrative investigation can be perceived by employees and we want to work with you to make the process as simple and expeditious as possible. The location and times of any interviews can be adjusted to meet your needs.

Your attendance and participation in this investigation is mandatory. You are directed to answer all questions posed by Lieutenant [name] and to be honest and forthright in your responses and are not to withhold any information. Failure to cooperate or provide truthful answers may subject you to discipline up to and including termination.

The complete interrogation will be video- and audio recorded. You will have access to the recording if any further proceedings are contemplated, or prior to any further interrogation at a subsequent time. You have the right to bring your own recording device and record any and all aspects of the interrogation.

You are advised that your rights are fully outlined in the Public Safety Procedural Bill of Right Act, Governance Code Sections 3300-3311. You have the right to have a representative of your choice present at all times during this interrogation. This representative shall not be a witness to the same investigation.

Allegation(s): It is alleged it on or around 5/20/16, you ordered an officer to change an accurate police report to match another officer's account of the same incident. The alleged conduct, if true, would be a violation of the following policies and city rules and regulations:

Walnut Creek Police Department Personnel Rules and Regulations:

Section 8 *Employee conduct*

Employees, either on duty or off duty, shall not engage in

conduct, which is of such nature that it causes discredit to the department.

City of Walnut Creek Rules and Regulations:

1202   CAUSE FOR DISCIPLINARY ACTION

> **m.** Violation of any of the provisions of these rules and regulations or departmental rules and regulations.
>
> **n.** Other behavior either during or outside of duty hours which is of such nature that it causes discredit to the City.

Lexipol Policies

341.5.8   PERFORMANCE

> **i.** Any act on or off duty that brings discredit to this department.

341.5.9   CONDUCT - Standards of Conduct

> **m.** Any other on or off-duty conduct which any member knows or reasonably should know is unbecoming a member of this department, is

contrary to good order, efficiency, or morale, or tends to reflect unfavorably upon this department or its members.

Personnel investigations follow accepted investigative practices. Investigators comply with requirements set

forth in Government Code 3300 et. seq; City of Walnut Creek Administrative Policy, current legal precedent, and applicable inter-agency protocols. If you have any concerns or questions about the Public Safety Officer's Procedural Bill of Rights, or about the complaint investigative process, please feel free to ask the investigator(s). Additionally, the Walnut Creek Police Management Association (PMA) may be available as a resource to their members who are involved in complaint investigations.

The city of Walnut Creek Rules and Regulations, all Department Policies (Lexipol), and WCPD Rules and Regulations for the alleged violations can be found on the Internet or the city Intranet.

[END OF LETTER]

Alleged Misconduct?? (based on what?) I am mandated to comply with an "Interrogation?" And possibly subjected to discipline, up to and including termination? For conduct that brings discredit to the

Walnut Creek Police Department, the City of Walnut Creek, and the entire profession of policing?

This was a career-ending betrayal from a group of people I thought were my family, my Tribe.

I hired an attorney and she told me not to communicate directly with them. She advised me that given their tone, all communications about my status should go through her from now on.

For those outside the law enforcement field, it's critical to understand that lying is a fire-able offense. From the minute we go to the Police Academy, we are told that any dishonesty is immediate grounds for termination. I once witnessed a highly decorated military veteran get kicked out of the police academy for stating something that was not truthful, even though it had no implications for anyone but himself. We are repeatedly drilled to understand that anyone who lies does not deserve to serve as a police officer. I had no history of anything like this, ever, in my many years of service. Lying is not something I had ever done either in the military or the police force.

Yet, all it took was one officer's baseless allegation to initiate a formal internal affairs investigation against me.

And the really messed up thing was that this other officer hadn't actually changed the thing in the report that he alleged I had told him to change. If I were his supervisor, and I told him to change something in the report, and he didn't do it, I wouldn't have signed off on it. So, the charge made no sense at all. This should have been a non-starter. But because of one officer's groundless allegation, I came under investigation, which delayed my retirement for most of a year.

This IA investigation came out of the blue, a month after I filed retirement paperwork. It called into question the character of my entire career with the Walnut Creek Police Department. My character had never been in question before within the department. It also put me at risk of being fired with no retirement benefits, of losing everything.

And here's an important detail to give further context: The officer who made this baseless allegation against me is the same person who had been investigated eight months earlier by the Walnut Creek Police Department. The charge? Multiple allegations of lying and *falsifying evidence in over 30 police reports.* This is a matter of both public record and the subject of several news reports at the time. If you Google his name, you'll be able to confirm this.

Here are a few excerpts from an article published on April 5, 2019, by Megan Cassidy of the San Francisco Chronicle:

A Walnut Creek police officer narrowly avoided being fired in 2017 after internal investigators found that he had mishandled evidence in dozens of cases…

…The probe into [Officer's name] began in early 2017, after internal investigators received information regarding [Officer's name] misrepresenting information in a police report…

In an April 18, 2017, letter, [Chief's name]…issued a scathing assessment of [Officer's name] conduct. "You have repeatedly proven yourself incompetent in the handling of evidence and completion of reports and raised serious questions about your honesty."[10]

Here are a few further excerpts from another article published around the same time:

"[Officer's name] made false entries about evidence in 31 police

---

10   Cassidy, M. (2019, April 5). Walnut Creek officer kept job after mishandling evidence in dozens of cases, report finds. San Francisco Chronicle. Accessed from

https://www.sfchronicle.com/crime/article/Report-Walnut-Creek-officer-kept-job-after-13746376.php *reports filed in 2015 and 2016, according to more than 860 pages of internal affairs reports by the Walnut Creek Police Department made public late Friday under Senate Bill 1421, the state's new police transparency law....*

Once you know that this Officer is behaving in this way and falsifying reports and mishandling evidence, (a review's) not limited to the cases that were discovered [public defender] Lipetsky said. There's an inference that he was probably doing the same types of things on every case he handled...

...but the Officer wasn't fired. Instead, Walnut Creek Police [Chief's name] gave him a "last chance" option.... "I do believe that the decision I made was made on the fact that he could be a credible officer, [Chief's name] said."[11]

In other words, when he was actively under internal investigation for a known pattern of falsifying reports, the accusing officer's baseless allegation was deemed sufficient cause to hold up my

---

11   Peele, T. and Lewis, S. (2019, April 8). Public Defender Calls for Case Review After Revelation of Walnut Creek Officer's Dishonesty. Bay Area News Group and KQED. Accessed from

https://www.kqed.org/news/11738567/public-defender-calls-for-case-review-after-revelation-of-walnut-creek-officers-dishonesty retirement for nearly a year. And, interestingly, despite multiple instances of falsifying his own reports and a very clear pattern of dishonest behavior, this officer was retained at the Police Department. In fact, this officer is still working at the Walnut Creek Police Department as of 2022.

Throughout the process of being investigated, I continually felt like my own "family" was attacking me. I had wanted to serve as a police officer from a very early age. It was a matter of my identity. Now my department was trying to ruin my reputation and make me lose everything. I felt like they had abandoned me. And once again, I felt like I was being treated like a criminal defendant.

I started to spin out of control again. I experienced the return of suicidal thoughts and feelings while I was under attack by my own department.

Thankfully, because of the work I had done in therapy, and what I had learned from trusted peers, I reached out to the safe people in my circles. I started to feel alone again, but I realized that I wasn't alone this time. Once, when my thoughts of despair felt overwhelming, I called the head peer coordinator for the West Coast Post Trauma Retreat. Nick and I talked for hours while I paced back and forth in my backyard. His support, and the support of others in my new healing community, grounded me and kept me from going into another full-blown crisis.

After nearly a year of waiting, the charges were dropped. Quite simply, there was no evidence to substantiate them. If not for my lawyer's continuous follow through, however, the Walnut Creek Police Department likely would not have informed me in a timely way that the charges had been dismissed. It was only when my lawyer continually followed up with them that they informed her there were no further charges against me. This was a reactive, rather than proactive response on the part of the Department, that came as a result of my lawyer's dogged persistence.

In Spring of 2018, she forwarded a single page letter from the Department that looked like this (exactly as written):

1. **Allegation:** WCPD Personnel Rules and Regulations, Section 8 – Employee Conduct.

Disposition: NOT SUSTAINED

2. **Allegation:** City Rules and Regulations Section 1202(m) – Causes for Disciplinary Action.

Disposition: NOT SUSTAINED

3. **Allegation:** City Rules and Regulations Section 1202(n) – Causes for Disciplinary Action.

Disposition: NOT SUSTAINED

4. **Allegation:** Lexipol Policy, 341, subsection 341.5.8 (i) – Standards of Conduct – Performance.

Disposition: NOT SUSTAINED

5. **Allegation:** Lexipol Policy, 341, subsection 341.5.9 (m) – Standards of Conduct – Conduct.

Disposition: NOT SUSTAINED

Based on this single sheet of paper, I was finally allowed to retire.

I never wanted to see or talk to any of these people again after this career-ending betrayal. But based on the good advice of someone I trusted, I decided to go back into the Police Department and finish things the hard way.

Doc Springer's Reflections

Navigating membership in particular groups (or Tribes) can be fairly complicated. Among law enforcement officers I've worked with, trust is often limited to one's immediate peers. There can be substantial distrust in some departments between officers and supervisors. But this wasn't really the case for Michael. He generally felt that his peers and supervisors were good people before this experience where he felt a sense of personal betrayal.

As Michael reminds us, he had always wanted to be a police officer, from a very young age. Serving in law enforcement had been part of his core identity. Law enforcement was the only career Michael really considered, and he had long been groomed to do the work, by his father Mike Gormley, who was also his personal mentor and hero.

In this particular case, Michael felt betrayed not just by a Captain (a senior law enforcement manager), but also by a subordinate officer who made an allegation against him that was totally unsubstantiated. Yet, despite this, Michael has never deviated from his deep respect for the profession as a whole. He continues to feel that the work is a noble calling. He believes in honesty, and in doing what is fair and right. He holds sacred a set of service-oriented values. Far from speaking negatively about police work, police departments, police officers, or department leaders, in the years after his retirement, he has poured himself into supporting first responders through their trauma. He has become a public advocate for getting law enforcement professionals and other first responders support for their trauma, despite systems that don't always work for them. He is still a Protector, just in a different way than before.

As he was telling me about these stories of betrayal, Michael didn't paint everyone with the same brush. There were leaders within his department who were kind, and supportive, even as they carried out the investigation. He noted another Captain who was straightforward and honest in all their dealings. Michael's issues with the particular Captain he references had to do with how he felt this Captain handled their interactions. From Michael's perspective, this Captain assumed that Michael would lie about being out of town, at Disneyland with his daughter.

I listened to the initial voicemail from the HR representative (a call that this Captain was present for). It was friendly, casual – even folksy – and did not convey any urgency whatsoever. Then I listened to the voicemail of the Captain the next day. This call had a completely different tone and a totally contrasting message from the initial call the day prior, some of which comes through in the words that were transcribed earlier in this chapter.

Michael immediately responded to that second call, having a very sensitive discussion about his work status, in the presence of his young daughter. Yet, the letter that arrived shortly thereafter somehow implied that he had not been responsive to the request for a timely return call.

It's hard to convey "tone of voice" when translating voicemails to words on a page. However, as an outside observer, I can see how Michael arrived at the conclusion that his Captain knew that he was at Disneyland, and was trying to trap him into a lie, which is a fire-able offense. After years of faithful service, and a history of strong performance, Michael's sense of betrayal was understandable.

For me, one of the main takeaways from this chapter was that if somebody is going to go on disability, or extended injury-related leave, the rules must be clear to both parties – the employer and the employee. Those whose employment status shifts must be informed of any rules and expectations, up front. Also, both parties need to have a good understanding of what the "on-ramp back into service" looks like and what a general time frame will be. Lack of clarity around this is fertile ground for breeding mutual mistrust and a variety of potential misperceptions about each other's motives, even in cases where both parties are acting in good faith.

Another key point to re-emphasize is that circles of trust are often very tight in professions like law enforcement and first responder communities, and in military service environments. The trust that forms between members of an "in group" is an important buffer to the trauma that individuals face in these lines of work. As Michael's story illustrates, law enforcement officers who work in patrol duties see a lot of trauma from things like domestic violence, drug operations, gang wars, sexual assaults, and suicide attempts. They trust each other with their lives as they go into fluid, highly dangerous situations. They sit in patrol cars for hours at times, just talking. They become "family" to each other. Individual identity becomes a group identity through this process.

As Michael was sharing his story for this chapter, he repeatedly made the point that the impact of on-the-job traumas and being personally attacked by his "law enforcement family" had a compounding effect. Michael talked about feelings of being "abandoned" but from my perspective – it went beyond abandonment. The allegations and charges made against Michael both questioned his character and suggested that he had discredited his department. Because of these allegations, he was in jeopardy of losing his job and his accrued retirement benefits. He was once again thrust into an investigative process where he had little power, and few personal rights. The feeling of his character and integrity being attacked during his lengthy legal battle after the fatal shooting would recur in this scenario. Once again, he would have felt like he was fighting to defend himself against personal attacks, but this time the source would be from inside his "law enforcement" family. For Michael, and perhaps others in the field, administrative betrayal can be the final piece that pushes officers over the edge. To suddenly be treated as an outsider who is viewed with suspicion rather than trust is devastating.

However, the critical thing to notice here is that this time, he was not alone. Because he had built out a network of safe and trusted people through confidential peer support circles, he still had a Tribe. Unlike before, this time, he didn't isolate and begin to drink heavily. When he started to feel suicidal, he noticed it immediately, and turned to someone he trusted. This person was a rock for him and helped anchor him during another perfect storm of stress. Without these kinds of relationships in place, it is much less likely that Michael would have survived this experience of feeling betrayed, abandoned and attacked.

It is my hope that Michael's work in this space of advocacy has improved, and will continue to improve, the situation for those who need to heal – so that they can return to duty in a way that preserves their dignity and respect. And even if policies are slow to change in some places, it is very clear that at our most painful and dangerous moments, when we connect, we survive.

13

LAST DAY

When we're traumatized, our natural human reaction is to disengage from the source of the trauma. We often want to sever ties and move on without looking back or being reminded of the pain. But in some cases, doing this can leave us with a feeling of having "unfinished business" for the foreseeable future. And this can impede our healing. Sometimes, the hard thing to do is the right thing in the long run.

In this chapter, Michael walks us through his last day at the Police Department.

***

Normally, when an officer retires, the Chief sends out a memorandum to everyone who works for the city of Walnut Creek. It's a career-defining moment where the Chief recognizes special assignments, awards, decorations, and that officer's years of honorable service. On his or her last day, there is a "walk out ceremony." Every employee, past and present, is invited to attend. As part of the walk out ceremony, the Chief publicly praises the officer for his or her achievements. It's like an extended wedding toast, but one where all the guests are invited to say a word of thanks or appreciation for that officer's time in service.

On an officer's last day, co-workers share stories – some hilarious, and some momentous – like the times they risked their lives together. Together they bask in these memories and favorite moments. The walk out ceremony is where the law enforcement family comes together to formally recognize one of its own. The goal is to send that person into retirement on a wave of appreciation, good will, and good humor. The day traditionally ends in several rounds of toasts at the local pub. There are few days in life where time is set aside for special recognition – in this communal way – and it's a day the retiring officer will never forget.

While I was on disability, I still had access to emails from the police department-wide "PD All" list-serve. A flood of emails came every day on topics like officer safety updates, personnel actions, shift reports, staffing issues, upcoming trainings, changes in teams – plus a wide variety of administrative messages. Initially, I was tracking shift reports, status updates and anything else that would help me stay up to date. I wanted to stay connected because my plan was to return to the department after I had healed.

Several months after I had gone on disability, my therapist recommended that I stop reading the department emails. She suggested that it was causing more harm than good. Specifically, it was causing me stress and anxiety from the continual feeling that I was missing out. I also felt a sense of guilt that I wasn't part of the team anymore. The hardest emails were the ones describing the shift reports of my old team, with a new supervisor. Those emails made me feel particularly guilty that I wasn't there for them. So, because of this, I agreed with my therapist, and deleted access to that email account, figuring I'd get caught up when I returned to duty.

And because I deleted this email account, when I did complete my retirement paperwork, I didn't receive the customary email that went out to every single city employee to share news of my retirement. However, a friend in the department sent me a screen shot. The entire message fit on the single small screen of my cell phone. It was just two lines, sent by the Chief to every city employee.

It read:

"Michael Sugrue is no longer employed by the city of Walnut Creek. We wish him well in his future endeavors."

My face suddenly got hot. My fists clenched up and I felt like my head was going to explode. My whole body got rigid, and I could almost feel the steam coming out of my nose. It was another punch in the gut after the betrayal of a ridiculous 11th hour IA investigation, with no evidence to support it.

I had risked my life on multiple occasions in the line of duty. I gave my all to the department, day in and day out, for 14 years. I didn't just respond to the calls of dispatch. I regularly took personal risks to assess situations that didn't feel right to me. I was proactive – fully committed to the mission of making the streets of Walnut Creek safer for residents, regardless of personal risk. I never took the easy path. I did my job to the standard of an Air Force Raven. The evidence of this was objectively verifiable - on every team I had been part of, I had made more self-initiated arrests than anyone else.

After 14 years of honorable, selfless service, the Chief sent a message to everyone I knew, and a lot of people I didn't know, that made it sound as though I had been fired.

The Chief's message had made it clear - that part of my life was done, and over. In the wake of yet another unbelievable administrative betrayal, I made a conscious decision: I would never set foot again in the department. I didn't want to answer peoples' questions. I already had a lot of fear, shame and embarrassment about transitioning to retirement – and now I had been publicly shamed as well.

Both the Chief and one of the two Captains in the Department had betrayed my trust. What they did – putting me through a baseless IA investigation that delayed my retirement, and then publicly shaming me with this city-wide email, hit me straight in the heart. I was so angry that I didn't know how I'd react if I ever had to face either of them again. For these reasons, my first instinct was to ask a fellow officer friend to box up my belongings and drop them off at my house.

But when I asked my friend Allen to collect my things, he told me that if I were to end things this way, I'd probably have regrets. After hearing him out, I decided to trust his advice. I resolved to return to the department, say my goodbyes, and pick up my things in person. I still had keys to the front door, but Allen had arranged to walk me through the entire process.

On the morning of this last day, as I dressed and had my coffee, I could feel my stomach twisting into a knot. While out on disability, I had avoided Walnut Creek, staying a safe distance from the location of my trauma and the people who had betrayed me. The knot in my stomach coiled tighter and tighter as I approached the city. I battled myself all the way in – fighting an intense urge to return home and ask my friend Allen to collect my things.

When I arrived, I pulled into the "visitor" parking lot. The urge to pull straight out again became overpowering. As soon as I put the car in "park," I scanned the lot for anyone I might recognize. I saw several familiar cars, which increased my anxiety. But then I saw Allen waiting for me, with a big smile on his face, and my anxiety dropped. I let out a breath I didn't know I was holding and stepped out of the car.

Allen had served as a reserve officer with me, like John Davison. We had trusted each other with our lives. I hadn't seen him in over a year and a half, having cut everyone off because it was too painful.

But when I saw him, I had an overwhelming feeling of relief as he gave me a big hug. Allen still cared about me. He still had my back. Some things don't change. And some people don't betray us – they just respect the distance we need.

As soon as we entered the department, we walked through a bullpen with several cubicles, where officers were working on reports. The people in that room showed mixed reactions to my presence. Some smiled in a genuinely kind and welcoming way. Others looked slightly confused by my appearance. Some showed irritation, and even fear. I had been a tough supervisor for some of them.

When I was last on duty, my picture was on the wall - part of the "status board" as the lead of a patrol team. But now, there was a picture of another sergeant on the wall, the new lead supervisor of my team. That was the moment I fully realized it: this is not my team anymore.

In the mail room, I looked through the names of the officers currently on duty. I was surprised that I didn't recognize most of them anymore. During the time I was away, there had clearly been a lot of turnover.

When I opened my mailbox, I found the picture of myself - the one that had previously been on the "status board" with my former patrol team. *When had it been placed there? When had I been replaced and written off?*

The next person I saw on my farewell tour was a kind man named John - a different John than my friend who served as a reserve officer. This John was a civilian that arranged our professional trainings. Because I had been a supervising sergeant, I had worked closely with him to line up several trainings for my team.

He was also the emcee every year for our retirement dinners. He leaned in close to me and said, "It's good to see you. How are you, Michael? I want you to know that I'm going to order you a retirement badge."

Here's the context for this, given the history in the department. In addition to their "last day walkout ceremony," retiring officers are also invited to attend a special dinner to honor all the retirees for that year. It happens once a year and it's a big deal. Because the honorees have retired throughout the past year, it's both a reunion and a celebration of anyone who used to work for the department. As part of this process, honorees are given a retirement badge. But historically, people who medically retire don't attend the dinner and they are not given a retirement badge. The message is this: If you are medically retired, these honors are *not for you.*

The fact that John had ordered me a retirement badge mattered. It showed me that I had had a positive impact on people in the department.

Next, I went to my private office space, where my rank had given me the best corner before I went out on disability. I expected to carefully pack my personal belongings. I needed this ritual as part of letting go of this period of my life. In my office were many things that were irreplaceable to me – objects that reminded me of my time as an Air Force Raven, and deeply personal things like pictures of my daughter. When I arrived, there was nothing there – nothing but a pile of boxes stacked on a pushcart. Some unknown person had invaded my privacy. I couldn't even confirm that everything was accounted for because it was already boxed up.
Who went through all my shit?! Another betrayal.

In light of the Internal Affairs Investigation, I started going down a rabbit hole again. *What were they looking for? Were they fishing for something that might incriminate me in the IA investigation they dropped on me after I filed my retirement paperwork? Were they trying to find something else they could use to hold up or deny my retirement? Why did I suddenly become someone they didn't trust?*

Why were they not decent enough to let me pack up my own things?
Even a criminal receives transparent accounting for the return of
their personal belongings when they're released from prison.

I pulled myself out of this mental tailspin and walked out of my
office. Next, I visited with the people in the record-keeping
department. Several of them stood up and hugged me. I needed
this, badly. I needed the reminder that there were people who
genuinely cared about me in the department. Their response also
confirmed that it was the right decision to say goodbye in person.
As hard as it was, Allen was right – I would've had regrets if I hadn't
done this.

After leaving record keeping, I ran into the Chief in the hall. This
was the moment I had been dreading. He said something that
struck me as lame and fake - something suggesting that he had no
clue about my suffering. I uttered a quick reply, equally meaningless
I'm sure, and moved past him.

My next stop was to pick up the things in my personal footlocker.
This time, I was able to go through the ceremony I had wanted
before, in my office space. I lovingly packed up the pictures of my
daughter Addy that were taped to the wall of my locker. I looked at
the row of uniforms neatly pressed and hanging up, waiting for my

return to duty. Part of me really wanted to keep my uniforms. They represented a core part of my identity. But anger and resentment were at war inside of me, and the other part of me wanted to just throw it all away, as I felt I had been thrown away.

The pain and anger won out this time.

I threw away three pairs of boots and turned in my weapons, magazines, ammo, tasers, gas masks, and riot helmet. I placed all my uniforms on a rolling garment rack and left them out for other officers to take. We did this for each other sometimes when we retired. It saves people money to take a uniform that fits them and change out the name and the patches. In retrospect, I wish I had kept at least one full duty uniform. The only one I kept was my honor guard uniform. This was the one I wore to funerals of fallen officers. Otherwise, I donated all of them.

I then moved on to visit with the other department Captain – not the one who had betrayed me, but the one I still felt cared about me. I sat in his office, and we had a heart-to-heart conversation. I told him how I had been struggling. I made it clear that I didn't plan on going out like this. I reminded him that I had wanted to be Chief someday and was on a fast track to this goal. I told him how angry I was about how the other Captain had treated me. I really wanted him to open up to me, and to empathize with me, but he wasn't able to do that. Still, it felt better to get it off my chest than to hold it all in. I felt secure in the fact that he cared about me, but he was also close friends with the Captain who had betrayed my trust, so he wasn't able to express his feelings openly with me.

After this last meeting on my last day, I rejoined Allen, who helped me carry all my belongings to my car.

At the end of this last day, there was no walkout ceremony, no public acknowledgement of my fourteen years of service. It was just me and Allen, and a rolling cart, pushing a pile of boxes to a parking spot in the "visitor" part of the lot.

Doc Springer's Reflections

In my most recent book, *WARRIOR: How to Support Those Who Protect Us,* I reflected on a curious phenomenon I've observed within the warrior community. I call it "hate at first sight." Think of "hate at first sight" as the opposite of "love at first sight." It's an explosive feeling of intense dislike of someone else – often paired with an urge to rough them up. Relationships among those in the military sometimes start with a no-holds-barred fist fight. At the same time, in many cases, these relationships often suddenly shift into an intense bond.

Case in point - when I was speaking to a group of more than two hundred active-duty Marines, I asked them, "How many of you hated on sight another Marine you now love like a brother and would trust with your life?" Hands shot up all over the room. It seems that it's not uncommon for service members who love each other like family to grow their relationship on a foundation of hate. The logical conclusion to draw from this observation is that the trust formed between service members is not necessarily a result of compatible or similar personalities.

To take this logic further, if baseline personality factors don't explain the love and trust that develops, then trust must be largely based on shared military culture and experiences. In other words, the experience of military service forges an indescribably deep bond of trust, creating a sense of Tribe, even between people who have vastly different personalities and personal values.

What develops this kind of trust? Like many things, it's multicausal, but some of the major factors include the resocialization of service members, a common language, a unique set of group experiences, a shared mission, and a shift away from individual to collective identity.

The same principle applies to the law enforcement Tribe. The context and the situation produce intense feelings of closeness and trust, or just the opposite. One of the important and unique things about both the military and the LEO community is the nature of these bonds. What people in these circles feel is deep belonging – or just the opposite. In other words, you are either IN, or you are OUT. Within these communities, there are further sub-groups where you are IN or you are OUT. In the LEO community, for example, you might be "in" with those who patrol the streets but have a general, shared distrust of those in administrative roles (Chiefs/Captains).

For fourteen years, Michael was "in" with both his fellow officers and his leadership. He was consistently and quickly promoted, and he excelled at his job, as one might expect from an Air Force Raven. Michael explained to me that within law enforcement, there are many good officers who do their jobs. They respond to calls from dispatch, and they perform their jobs competently. There are others though who take to the work at an entirely different level. Michael explained that these officers actively seek to keep the streets safer, regardless of personal risk.

I asked Michael for an example, and he talked about the scenario of an officer at the end of his or her shift who notices suspicious activity on the way back to the department. It's been a long shift and he or she wants to get home. One officer might disregard the suspicious activity, rationalizing that it's probably not a criminal issue. Another will stop and assess the situation, even if this creates personal risk and leads to an arrest, hours of overtime, and extra paperwork. Michael impressed on me that he was consistently the latter type of person. Leading his teams in self-initiated arrests is how this difference showed up in performance metrics. This is the reason he was fast-tracked over the fourteen years he served in the department.

Throughout the process of hearing and writing up Michael's story, I've worked to convey his emotional response to the traumas he's faced. To understand these, it is critical to continually remember that law enforcement was not a job for Michael – it was the core of his identity. In this chapter, when he talks about feeling "replaced" on his old team or discovering that someone unceremoniously packed up his personal items, he is expressing the pain of feeling like an outsider in a Tribe that felt like family at one time.

What did he do to deserve this? Nothing. It's what happens in some departments when an officer goes out on disability. Someone who has earned 14 years of trust can suddenly feel like an outsider and be treated as though they are not trustworthy. Sometimes "families" are most brutal to their own. And until this culture shifts, there will be officers who are gravely wounded, who continue to compartmentalize their pain, at risk to themselves and others, as they suffer in silence over many years. An often-overlooked barrier to treatment is the fear of being pushed out of their Tribe if they ask for help on the record – that in the final days of their time in service, it will be "hate at last sight" followed by a permanent removal from membership in the group.

Here's another key insight I want to re-emphasize. It would be harder for many law enforcement professionals to show up for a "last day" like Michael's than to run into a drug house filled with armed criminals. Michael talked about "battling" himself all the way in, on the drive back to the department. It would have been far easier to ask Allen to get his things and wipe his hands of this entire chapter of his life. This was his original plan. But it was the kindness of his friend Allen that made the difference in the end. Allen shared wise counsel when he told Michael that he should say his good-byes in person. And Allen showed up to give him the moral support he needed to step out of the car and go through that process.

What I hoped to convey in this chapter was how mixed this experience was for Michael. Michael's last day in the department was an emotional bender of high and low moments, all in rapid succession: Allen's welcoming embrace, the mixed reactions of his fellow officers, finding his photo removed from the wall, John's insistence on ordering Michael a retirement badge, discovering his office boxed up and sitting on a rolling cart, people that expressed genuine care for him, the meaningless words spoken by the Chief in a hurried utterance, the ceremony of cleaning out his locker for the last time, giving away his duty uniforms, the interaction with the Captain who did care about him, and ending the day as it had begun – just Michael and Allen, parting in friendship and mutual respect.

The painful experiences and interactions were interspersed with moments of genuine connection. These are moments Michael wouldn't have had if he had taken the easy path. Michael would be the first to acknowledge that Allen was right – if he hadn't gone to the department in person, he would have had regrets.

Keeping a "safe" distance would have allowed suspicion and mistrust to go unchecked and unanswered. Retreating as though he was guilty of some wrongdoing would have taken a toll on Michael in time. He would not have had the chance to look people in the eyes, and to give and receive the parting of mutual respect that he needed. Michael was denied the customary "walk out ceremony" but there were moments of the day that filled this need for closure. Most of all, Michael was able to meet this adversity on his own terms. Doing this was harder than doing the work required during his years of patrol. Nonetheless, he faced his fears and walked through this day.

Based on my observations of similar scenarios, I'm confident that Michael's healing journey would have been more difficult if he had taken the avoidant path. The right path is not always the easy path.

14

HEALING

In this chapter, Michael reflects on the choices, people, programs, and treatments that have been critical for his healing journey.

***

(About 10 months later)

Out of the blue, I got a message from a man named Danny Burde. Danny hosts a podcast called "Iron Crew" – which is focused on fitness topics, including exercise, nutrition, and wellness. For several months, I had been posting messages on LinkedIn to support mental health awareness for veterans and first responders.

Danny had been reading my posts. He wanted to interview me for his podcast.

When I got Danny's message, I felt flattered that he asked, but I was uncomfortable with his request. With the exception of sharing my story with my therapist, or with people in the confidential West Coast Post Trauma Retreat, sharing my story publicly had not gone well. I'd been damaged by the media when several journalists had published wildly inaccurate theories of what happened on the night of the shooting and everything that followed. As I mentioned previously, when you're involved in an active legal case, especially as an officer of the law, you can't comment or otherwise correct the record. Being subjected to these news stories brought additional trauma into my life. The publication of these speculative news stories left me feeling helpless and undefended.

As part of the legal process, I had been compelled to give depositions with cameras in my face and hostile attorneys trying to trip me up. I had also been forced to publicly testify, while everything I had was in jeopardy – my reputation, my career, my financial future. More than once, I had broken down sobbing in front of everyone present. So, no thanks, I wasn't going to go on a podcast and share my story.

I politely declined Danny's interview request. He didn't give up. He emailed me two more times, each time insisting that it would really help a lot of people if I could share my story. He told me that he was willing to drive to me to make it happen.

In January 2019, I agreed to meet up with him for what I thought would be an initial exploratory conversation. As we agreed, I met him at my local Mimi's Café, thinking we'd sit down and get to know each other over breakfast. I showed up in a blue sweatshirt and jeans, the hair on my face grown into a full beard at this point. I was not ready for an interview. Frankly, I showed up just to be polite.

When I arrived, I found that he had reserved the private room in the back of the restaurant. Spread across a large booth was a laptop and his A/V set up, two sets of headphones and a camera set up on poles. This was a familiar scene - reminiscent of depositions and court room proceedings, but it felt different that day.

Using my professionally honed ability to size people up, I could tell that he was not there to trap me. He really wanted to support me. I could see the compassion and warmth in his eyes. He had driven an hour and a half for this meeting. His window of availability was only an hour and a half so unfortunately, we only had time for the interview itself - no pre-interview discussion.

My gut told me to go with the flow. Instead of sitting down for breakfast, I seated myself across from him in the booth and we started the interview.

My initial anxiety about the podcast faded as I started sharing my story. I stayed focused on Danny and his intent, which was to give me a supportive place to tell my story. It all came flooding back to me, and I went with it, without holding back. My anxiety disappeared. The words and thoughts came without effort.

It takes a few weeks to produce a podcast. Before my episode was released, there were times when I worried about what would happen once it published. There would be no going back at that point – no way to conceal what I was feeling and thinking. My trauma would be "out there" for everyone to hear.

Would people judge me?

Would my former colleagues listen to it or not?

Would Anthony Banta's family hear it? How would they feel about it?

When the podcast came out, I was surprised by my own reaction. When I listened to it, there wasn't anything I regretted saying, even though I had been an open book. It felt entirely different from how I had told the story before.

When I had shared my story before in the court room, I was acutely traumatized, with no one in my corner after my dad died. I was alone in that courtroom, and my character was repeatedly attacked. During these attacks by Banta's legal team, I was legally compelled to answer their questions – even the distorted and demeaning ones. This was totally different.

When the podcast published, I was further surprised to get a flood of messages from all over the world. Complete strangers applauded me for sharing my story so openly. Several of them said that my story had helped them recognize where they were struggling. They started sharing their stories in response. I could feel their hope rise as they too opened up about their pain. They didn't feel alone because of what I shared. And I no longer felt alone either. I started to see how sharing my story had been courageous.

I also had friends and colleagues reach out repeatedly. As a theme, they told me they had no idea I was going through this. My family and friends supported me.

Though I was initially resistant to the interview, Danny Burde's persistence resulted in an experience that infused a sense of purpose in me - purpose I had not felt since I had retired from the police department.

So, I had a new purpose, but does that mean that I was "cured" from my post-traumatic stress? No.

Healing is an ongoing thing. However, I've been fortunate to attend and benefit from some amazing programs and treatments that have been critical in my healing journey.

The West Coast Post Trauma Retreat, mentioned earlier in the book, has been a consistent part of my healing. When I first entered West Coast Post-Trauma Retreat, I was in bad shape, full of anxiety and fearful of sharing my story.

For fourteen years, I had been exposed to trauma after trauma in my work as a police sergeant, but I hadn't talked about any of it. When the really bad stuff happened, we made a joke about it and just kept going. No one, including myself, had revealed how these traumas were taking a toll on us. We were afraid that we'd be perceived as the odd man out if we did. We were afraid that people would look at us differently, trust us a little less, hold back on promoting us when the time came.

At West Coast Post Trauma Retreat, I met other men and women that I could identify with. Because they modeled open sharing, and because I respected them, I could be vulnerable in return. When I did open up to them, they received my story with respect. Because I had such difficulty with trust, I didn't go all in the first time I went to the West Coast Post Trauma Retreat, but even so, I didn't want to leave at the end of that week. It felt incredible to have a safe place to talk about Trauma. I didn't want to return to the outside world yet.

One of the great things about the program is that they don't just support you for a week and then drop you back into normal life. The program opens you up and lays the foundation for the things you need to work on. The "work" of navigating the changes and stressors that life brings is ongoing. The peer volunteers help you develop longer term plans that help you set goals for 90 days, 6 months, 1 year, 3 years, and 10 years out. The program includes post-retreat Zoom meetings – optional, but really valuable – to help each cohort make progress on their personal growth goals.

I've remained involved with the program, now in the role of a peer volunteer. It's ironic because I was so reluctant to share at first. Now, I get to help set the culture of the program and create a safe space for others to start their healing journeys. Along with the other peer volunteers, I help facilitate the morning check-ins and other meetings throughout the day. One of my favorite meetings is

"Chapel" – a non-religious, spiritually focused gathering. For example, a question we might all reflect on during a "Chapel" meeting is, "What comes to mind when you think of forgiveness?"

Sometimes in our recovery process, it's hard to see how far we've come. One of the unexpected benefits of staying connected to the program is that I can see how far I've come. I can see an earlier version of myself in those who first join the program, and I get to see how people grow through their trauma. I encourage them to take full advantage of the program – to go "all in" and share their stories without fear of losing respect. We help each other grow – for example, by talking about how we manage our triggers and how we use strategies to get better sleep. And now, as the weeklong program ends, instead of dreading returning to "real life," I look forward to the people and good things that await me at home.

Another program that has helped me is called "Save-A-Warrior." It is also about five days long and it's geared for veterans and first responders. However, the focus is not on combat trauma or first responder trauma, but on childhood trauma. I didn't identify as someone who had childhood trauma at first, but when I spoke to the intake coordinator, he said, "We need to get you here. You need this."

When I arrived, there was a group of men sitting in a room, disconnected, anxious, and uncomfortable in each other's presence. But as the program played out, they began to open up about their experiences – a wide range of childhood trauma like being molested, beaten by a caregiver, or abandoned.

Hearing their stories helped me realize how much the issues of abandonment and betrayal had shaped my life. These themes helped me see how my first responder trauma had impacted me. Abandonment and betrayal summed up the experience I had in the courtroom and with some police department leaders.

When I gained this insight, further healing became possible. Both my biological father and my stepfather had died in the same sudden, cruel way from the same form of cancer. However, when my biological father had died, we were estranged. Our last conversation was painful. When I fully connected to the impact of abandonment and betrayal in my life, instead of blaming my biological father for my feeling of abandonment, I started to see him as a victim of his own trauma. This was critical because it helped me find compassion for him.

Even though he was gone, I was able to reconnect with positive memories of him through a powerful ritual called "the ceremony for the dead." During the ceremony, I forgave my dad and told him how much I loved and missed him. This provided critical healing that I needed.

In 2021, I also had the opportunity to receive Stellate Ganglion Block (SGB). It first came up during one of the phone calls I had with Doc Springer, as we were talking through my trauma for this book. To be honest, I was really skeptical at first. But Doc and I built a deep trust and I kept seeing people post things on LinkedIn about how they had responded to SGB.

What ultimately convinced me was a conversation I had with an Air Force veteran name Chris Jachimiec. Chris had gone through a treatment that combined Stellate Ganglion Block with a wellness program at Mission 22 called "Recovery + Resiliency." The program empowers veterans to heal with the benefit of ongoing support. The "R+R" program is several months long, and it includes wellness coaching, a membership to a community-based fitness experience (like CrossFit), nutritional supplements, and biometric devices. For example, everyone in the program is given a Garmin watch that provides data on their sleep quality and heart rate variability. Participants also receive a lifetime membership to NuCalm, a biometric device that aids with daily meditation.

When I talked with Doc about the SGB, she had explained that SGB should not be seen as a standalone treatment, but done in combination with a program like "R+R." My conversation with Chris – who had done SGB in combination with "R+R" really locked in this insight.

Doc was with me when I went to the clinic to get SGB which meant a lot to me. I knew that nothing would go wrong because she was there to provide overwatch.

The procedure was quick and painless. The nurses and the doctor at the clinic were phenomenal. They explained everything and it was over before I knew it. We went out to eat afterwards. The food tasted amazing. Until Doc brought it to my attention, it didn't occur to me that I had sat with my back to an entire crowded restaurant of people without once thinking about it. I just sat down and enjoyed the food and the conversation, without any distractions or anxiety. That night I slept well, and I woke up feeling rested for the first time in a long time.

After the procedure, I've felt less on edge. Normally, I get easily upset by reckless drivers, and have struggled for many years with road rage. But after the SGB, I notice that I've felt much more relaxed when driving my car, and I'm much less agitated by drivers speeding past me or cutting me off. I've also noticed that SGB has improved my focus, particularly when I'm working out. My friends at the gym have commented on this too. I didn't feel the sudden release of emotions that other people sometimes report, but SGB has made me feel less agitated and less annoyed overall.

So SGB has also been an important part of my healing, in combination with Mission 22's program. I am now meditating every day. I am living intentionally now, in a way that promotes mental and emotional wellness. I have a sense of purpose in the work I do as an advocate and speaker to help first responders. I get to help others see that there is hope and healing for their trauma. It's not the mission I first saw when I entered the police department, but it's one that allows me to fully live into my deepest sense of purpose and meaning. I absolutely enjoy my time with the people I love – and anytime I am with my daughter Addy is a great day. I am at peace, and happy to be alive.

Doc Springer's Reflections

As Michael was talking about his healing process, three things jumped out to me. First, I want to pin down the difference between traumatizing sharing and therapeutic sharing. They are both "sharing" your story, but the outcome is completely different. Michael experienced both in the extreme. One deepens the impact of trauma, while the other heals us.

In the former category, the "sharing" that Michael did as part of his courtroom proceedings added trauma upon trauma. Let's remember that there were moments where he once thought this sharing might be helpful. For example, at the coroner's inquest, he hoped that maybe his ex-wife would be able to understand his pain when he shared his story. He hadn't been able to fully open up to her previously. But telling her all the details in this way, and in this environment, was neither therapeutic, nor helpful to their relationship.

The "sharing" that Michael did during legal depositions and as part of courtroom testimony is a great example of the polar opposite of "emotional safety." Michael was legally compelled to respond to all questions – even those designed to trick him or trip him up – while his future hung in the balance. Sharing his testimony was required by law, but let's be clear that this process was highly traumatic for him, as it would be for anyone else.

The critical point is this: just "sharing our story" isn't what heals us – in some cases, sharing can deepen our wounds. The kind of sharing that heals us meets three conditions. All three are necessary for sharing to be helpful instead of harmful.

First, the trauma survivor must be in the right "mind state" while sharing. The trauma by itself is enough of a challenge – and will create anxiety for most people as they begin to share. What needs to be eliminated is extra, unnecessary fear – a second layer of anxiety about the costs of opening up. It is essential for survivors to share without fear of consequences – to their jobs, their acquired professional rank, their financial status, their reputation, and their family situation. Otherwise, they'll be sharing their story while feeling primal fear.

To return to the central theme in my previous book, *WARRIOR*, healers must build the kind of trust that invites the full story to emerge. The first story that trauma survivors tell is often a test of trust. Can a healer or peer supporter be trusted to hear the *deeper* pain that is eating them alive, silently, privately? The story of people's hidden pain is the truth that begins to set them free. This story will emerge when the storyteller is in the right mind state.

Second, a survivor must have sufficient control over the timing and conditions for sharing their story. If a healer or peer supporter sets a condition that pressures the storyteller to open up before they feel safe, it's not likely to be therapeutic. Admittedly, when Michael showed up at Mimi's Café, there was a degree of pressure to do the interview, but Michael could have declined to proceed. Based on his interactions with Danny and his assessment of Danny's motives, Michael felt sufficient control and comfort to move forward.

Some types of therapy compel detailed sharing of trauma experiences before trust has been built. Again, to return to a theme I cover extensively in my book *WARRIOR*, professional healers often make the mistake of assuming that their education and licensure are sufficient to create trust with all their patients. This may be the case for some populations. When I was in private practice, working with a civilian population, my Harvard and University of Florida degrees on my office wall set a condition of trust for the majority of my patients. They looked forward to therapy, opened up with a high degree of comfort, and together we moved them through their challenges. For some populations, though, spending many years in school doesn't bridge the trust gap – it widens it.

The academic world is far removed from the gritty realities of trauma – for example, in a warzone, or in crime-ridden cities. Some survivors believe that people who spend many years in graduate school lack "real world" understanding (and, unfortunately, sometimes they're right). In any case, assuming a trust that hasn't been earned will backfire. And if the therapist moves too fast in pushing patients to disclose their trauma, they will break the trust and cause harm to those they intend to support. The patient must be in the driver's seat. The patient must feel in control and empowered to lead the process as they share their story. This is critical for healing to occur.

Third, the story must be told in the right environment. The "right" environment is one that seasoned healers may refer to as a "therapeutic container." A "therapeutic container" is a radically safe space – physically and emotionally. The storyteller needs to feel that whatever he or she shares will not meet with a reaction of shock, horror, fear, blame, or personal judgment of any kind.

The healer's ability to respond in an open, kind-hearted, compassionate way is critical. A true healer is capable of walking through the trenches of mental warfare, as a trusted guide, but never a "savior." When circles of peers become healers, they must be similarly well prepared to receive trauma stories, in a place of radical safety. Michael's experience with West Coast Post Trauma Retreat is a great example of what "right" looks like.

A second general theme I want to pull out from this chapter is the importance of modeling. A friend of mine from graduate school once shared this statement: "Mentoring is modeling." So true. If people lack a model for what healing looks like, what we ask them to do in therapy can be a bridge too far. This is why peer support is a critical part of recovering, in addition to working with a skilled professional healer. People who serve in certain professions, such as law enforcement, often lack examples of how people can heal. Therapeutic sharing is not part of their culture. It's just the opposite. As Michael explained in an earlier chapter, "gallows humor" is the way that people cope with their pain. And as I reflected earlier, this response is understandable, and even helpful, in the short run. But it's not sufficient to stem the tide of trauma upon trauma. The unspeakable things must be spoken, and reckoned with directly, in healing spaces.

As an unwritten rule, those in our military and first responder communities are united by a culture of stoicism. In other words, they suffer in silence, holding a poisonous level of trauma that often goes unaddressed for many years. They often lack examples of strong, brave people talking with complete candor about the things that burn them with shame, or the things that are breaking them down inside. Without these kinds of examples, it's harder for any patient to derive the full benefit of professional therapy.

But when people have the benefit of participating in safe circles of peers, they can see what it looks and feels like for people to share without losing respect. They can see responses that preserve the dignity of those who share their pain. A veil is lifted, and healing becomes possible, both in these peer circles, and with the benefit of trusted professional healers. This is why no one should ever pit "peer support" against "professional help" and ask a question like "which is better?" These modes of healing are _fundamentally complementary._ Peer support and professional therapy are both effective and doing both at the same time can be powerful, as long as everyone aligns their support.

The final take-away I want to draw out is the myth of "one right treatment" for all people. As Michael's story shows, healing is an ongoing journey. Personally, I've seen more growth from my patients when we tackled specific issues with intensity over short periods of time, with breaks in between. Therapy is hard work and setting a cadence for growth can be an intentional process. As an unapologetically "free range" psychologist, I have never felt that one treatment is best for every patient. People are complex. Different people may need different interventions to heal. The same person may need to pursue a few different programs, as Michael did, to achieve sustained wellness. Each of the programs and treatments Michael received, therapy with a skilled professional healer, the West Coast Post Trauma Retreat, Save-A-Warrior, Mission 22's "R+R" program, and Stella's Stellate Ganglion Block treatment helped Michael "level up" his healing as my friend Dayna Wolter would put it.

When someone is referred to a healing program, there can be an assumption that "graduation" indicates that someone has achieved healing. This is another misleading notion. Healing is possible, but "wellness" is a fluid thing that ebbs and flows over time - for all of us.

At the same time, in the past few years, one of the most important revelations I've had, as a trauma psychologist, is this: the fusion of biological and psychological treatments is uniquely powerful to support healing. Stellate Ganglion Block (SGB) is one of the most promising interventions for psychological trauma. SGB involves injecting a widely available, commonly used anesthetic medication into a bundle of nerves in the neck, called the "stellate ganglion," just above the collarbone. Performed on an outpatient basis, a typical procedure takes about 15 minutes. When performed by a properly trained doctor, SGB is considered a safe, routine procedure.

While many in the mental health field are not yet familiar with SGB, it is not a "new" treatment. SGB has been used to treat pain related diagnoses for nearly a century – including shingles, complex regional pain syndrome, and phantom limb pain. It has been used to treat Post-Traumatic Stress symptoms in military hospitals, special forces units and select VA treatment facilities. Thousands of warfighters have gotten relief from their worst symptoms of trauma with this procedure, usually within a single session.

Using SGB to treat traumatic stress symptoms requires adopting a new treatment model. Rather than being seen as purely a "psychological" condition, post-traumatic stress is also seen as a biological injury. This is important for two reasons. First, for many who suffer, the term "disorder" has a stigma attached to it. On the other hand, an "injury" is widely seen as a no-fault, no-shame challenge, without any associated stigma. Second, the concept of a "disorder" often suggests a more permanent condition. A disorder is more likely to influence a person's core identity. In contrast, an "injury" is often seen as treatable with the right intervention. We often manage "disorders," while we _heal_ from "injuries."

The "injury" model suggests that trauma is largely a biological condition, with paired psychological and social components. In other words, trauma causes an involuntary, physiological change, that can leave us stuck in "fight or flight" mode. After exposure to trauma, we may have recurrent challenges like disrupted sleep, anger attacks, overwhelming panic, difficulties concentrating, a feeling of constantly being on "high alert", and a strong startle response - in other words, the "hyper-arousal" cluster of trauma symptoms. I refer to this state as "chronic threat response" in my previous work and writing.

The accumulation of hyperarousal symptoms is a _common occupational hazard_ for individuals in certain professions – such as police officers, firefighters, EMTs, dispatchers, combat flight nurses, and ER workers who treat dying patients. SGB can offer relief for the symptoms associated with chronically high stress or trauma exposure that is a routine part of these occupations.

When SGB is used in combination with psychotherapy and other mind-body wellness practices, its full power is unleashed. SGB and therapy have a reciprocal enhancement effect. As Arturo Weber, a Marine treated with SGB put it, SGB is the "primer" before the "paint" of psychotherapy and other wellness programs.

To understand how this works, it's key to observe how a chronically over-activated "fight or flight" system impedes good therapy outcomes. As many patients and therapists have noted, psychotherapy requires complex mental work. At the same time, trauma fragments our ability to focus and makes it very hard to concentrate.

However, when our minds and bodies are calm again, new insights flow more easily. Patients who feel relaxed in their bodies are more willing and able to talk about their trauma. Feeling in control again in their bodies helps them develop new behaviors that promote long-lasting recovery. They move forward with confidence and a sense of empowerment, and they readily gain a new understanding of their trauma.

This is a critical point – *peoples' identities begin to shift the moment they experience relief of their symptoms.* This positive shift comes from the realization that they are *not broken,* that they can heal, and that *post-traumatic stress is not a life sentence.* I have seen countless patients experience this kind of transformation of mind and body. This is why I believe that SGB should be offered as a first line treatment, to anyone suffering from trauma symptoms who wants it. To ask anyone to wait when we are losing irreplaceable people to suicide every day is unconscionable. And to force those who suffer to "fail" other therapies first makes no sense. It's not patient-centric or compassionate, and it misses the point. Innovation lies in the fusion of biological and psychological treatments, and the sequencing of these matters. In other words, we need to treat the biological injury, and then provide the right insights and the right psychological support. This new model for treatment is what I see as the way forward, for the field of trauma care.

The work of skilled psychologists, social workers, mental health counselors, wellness coaches, and mind-body practitioners remains critical to this process. In this way, Stellate Ganglion Block, used in combination with high quality mental health support, brings new promise as a safe, efficacious, accelerated path to recovery.

SGB has real promise when it comes to treating first responder trauma for several reasons –

- It removes the barrier of mental health stigma
- It usually works within minutes
- Downtime after a procedure is less than 24 hours
- It's not psychoactive (it carries no drug test risk)
- It has no negative impact on reaction time (reaction time can even be improved)
- It is 70-80% successful in reducing target symptoms across multiple studies
- It can be delivered in a confidential, efficient way

In the next, and final section, of the book, we'll zoom out and consider why healing the trauma of our first responders – using the best, most innovative methods available – is critical for their wellbeing and the wellbeing of our society.

THE FUTURE OF LAW ENFORCEMENT
ENFORCEMENT
A FINAL REFLECTION

THE FUTURE OF LAW ENFORCEMENT

A Word Before We Begin

When it comes to supporting communities of color and those who serve in law enforcement roles, there is incredible pressure to "choose a side." I cannot, and will not, choose a side. I am a trauma psychologist and I care deeply about both communities. Further, the line between these communities is fluid in my personal experience since many people in my network are members of both communities simultaneously.

Racism is one of society's oldest evils. It is a form of societal cancer.

The trauma sustained by those in communities of color is pervasive. We are all responsible for identifying racism and addressing it.

Sometimes, for example, in the case of wrongful deaths of African American citizens, we all become aware of egregious violations of an officer's duty to protect and defend. But most of the time, racial trauma is insidious. Racist behavior may be invisible to those of us who are not targeted because of our race. To be targeted in this way is to live under a constant sense of threat. And there are communities where the trust between civilians and police officers is broken.

Michael and I acknowledge this trauma.

As a trauma psychologist, my purpose is to shine light on the pain that causes deaths of despair, and other heart-breaking outcomes. For many years, I have served as a trusted Doc for our nation's warfighters and first responders. This has brought me into close contact with a Tribe of people – incredible men and women – who make selfless sacrifices to protect all of us. They face unimaginable traumas in the work they do. The human impact of these traumas has been invisible to most of us as well.

The scope of this book is to focus on trauma within the first responder community by delving into the particulars of one officer's experiences. In doing this, we are not choosing a side. All human pain needs a voice. We honor the pain of both communities, and hope that our work may play a role in bridging the divide that now exists.

—Doc Springer

Who should be the one to take the lead on writing a final reflection about the future of law-enforcement?

The obvious choice would be Michael. But the obvious choice doesn't feel right. It feels important for this chapter to be written by me, Doc Springer, as a civilian who has been brought into a much deeper understanding of what is happening among our law enforcement professionals.

Law enforcement professionals operate within a different sphere. What they see and do is largely unknown outside of their immediate circle. They engage in dangerous encounters, and may risk their lives while on duty, and most of the time, we never hear these stories. Their trauma is also hidden from us. I teamed up with Michael to make his trauma, and the trauma of so many of our first responders, visible.

Michael served as a police sergeant in the town I thought I knew. Walnut Creek is a wonderful place to live, to be sure. We enjoy very low crime, or at least, that used to be the case before the past two years. Even so, there is an underbelly to every city across the nation.

My conversations with Michael have opened my eyes to this element in my local community. I now know where drugs are likely to be sold, where sexual encounters between strangers are likely to take place, and which apartment complexes and foot massage spas have been fronts for prostitution. On the night when Michael was forced to take the life of an armed assailant, my family and I were safely sleeping less than 3 miles from where it happened.

I've gained a new understanding from being steeped in Michael's story for over a year. What I know comes directly from his relentless courage – the trust we hold with each other, his complete vulnerability, and his willingness to drop his emotional armor, and answer every question I asked him throughout this process. We did it to save lives.

For over a year, I've been reflecting on how Michael's story reflects larger trends in our society. In this chapter, I'll work to put some thoughts together. Michael will then share his final reflections as we close out this project.

While Michael's traumas are not unique, his vulnerability is very rare. He gives voice to not just the trauma, but the sense of abandonment and betrayal he felt in the aftermath of trauma. In this chapter, we reflect on our society's changing perceptions of those in law enforcement roles and what may help us bridge the divide that now exists.

✳✳

If we are to understand the current state of law enforcement, the first question we should ask is this: Does evil actually exist?

If it doesn't, and everybody who engages in crime just needs healing or resources, perhaps we should defund the police, and bring in an army of psychologists and social workers instead of armed officers.

Some people appear to hold this kind of view.

The problem is: our army of healers would get laughed at, or picked off, on the streets if we did. Because evil DOES EXIST.

Michael saw the face of evil, or its after-effects during a portion of his calls, as he shares in previous chapters. And I fully agree that evil exists, based on my general background as a psychologist, and my unique role as a trusted Doc to our nation's warfighters and first responders.

Evil exists.

There is a subset of people that take pleasure in harming others. Some of them delight in doing evil. There are also those among us who are singularly motivated towards personal gain regardless of how many lives they destroy. In the field of psychology, we may classify this as "antisocial personality disorder." I've encountered these people in my work. It's a chilling experience to lock eyes with someone with dead eyes, who looks at you merely as an object.

Combat warfighters also have the credibility to help us understand that evil exists. My friend Jason Tuschen, a Navy SEAL leader, is one of the kindest people I know. Before going into the military, he took joy in being a chef at a hibachi restaurant, cooking delicious meals and making people laugh in the process. Jason loves the ocean. He's a surfer. And he's somebody with a huge heart who is widely respected as a people-driven leader. Jason engaged in years of tireless effort to get his Iraqi interpreter, Johnny Walker, and JW's family, to safety. Jason was willing to risk his military career and his own freedom to get them out of Iraq.

Based on his experiences in war, here's what Jason said about the presence of evil – "There are some people who will twist the world to meet their perverse needs. These are people who just need to be stopped."

Some of Michael's stories carry the same truth. Evil lives among us and resides deep in the heart of some people. Michael would also be the first to say that not everyone who engages in criminal behavior is evil.

There is a second group of people who are not fundamentally evil. These people get caught up in law breaking behavior for different reasons. The young man in chapter 3 ("Near Death Experience") is a good example of this. He's a basically good kid who made a string of bad decisions. Michael was devastated by how close he came to firing his weapon at this kid, who is a good person at heart.

Some lawbreakers aren't driven by evil, but they are trapped in the stranglehold of addictions. They engage in criminal behavior to feed these addictions. There is another category of people who aren't actively looking to do criminal acts, but who become opportunistic if they think they won't get caught.

And here's the thing: there are the same exact categories of humanity within the police force.

Police are people, just like the rest of us. Within their ranks are represented the kinds of people I just described. While a minority, there are bad cops who abuse their power because they can. These are the people we must weed out of law enforcement. There's a second group that is trapped by addictions or other forms of private bondage, who misuse their power because they're not well. And there are officers who will be opportunistic if they see a way to get away with the perfect crime. In some parts of the country, and in some communities, there are systemic problems, and a trust that has been violated so many times that it's broken.

There are also countless law enforcement professionals who are honorable people, doing their best to serve and protect us. In my work with service members and first responders, I've seen the inherent goodness and the code of honor that is core to many who serve in these professions. Many of the best people I know, with the biggest hearts for service, are law enforcement professionals. As in Michael's case, to serve and protect, is what drew them to the career in the first place.

Criminal behavior also exists within a delicate ecosystem that has revealed itself in the past year and a half. Initially, during the pandemic, we were told that all forms of crime were down. This was true for several months, while we were in collective shock. Violent crime decreased in part because people were mostly sequestered at home. But after the initial drop in crime, we've seen a significant rise in non-violent criminal behavior, such as package thefts and car break-ins.

At the same time, we've seen efforts to defund the police, across the country. Proactive policing shows police presence and is a deterrent to crime. But as Michael explained, in today's police culture, any stop an officer makes can lead to the officer being sued. When officer proactivity is punished, the culture shifts from proactive to reactive engagement. In other words, instead of trying to prevent crime, police officers are increasingly activated only in response to crimes in progress.

To add to the mix, we are losing police, every day. We are losing many of them to suicide. In August 2021, the Washington Post published an article titled, "Death by suicide among police is a quiet epidemic. It needs to be acknowledged.[12]" Blue H.E.L.P., a non-profit that collects statistics on officer suicides, shows that this year alone, 116 law enforcement officers in the United States have died

---

12   Sourced 12/8/21 at: https://www.washingtonpost.com/local/death-by-suicide-among-police-is-a-quiet-epidemic-it-needs-to-be-acknowl-edged/2021/08/09/c7dc2036-f941-11eb-9c0e-97e29906a970_story.html

by suicide as of December 1, 2021.[13]

To put this into context, more officers die by suicide each year than are killed in the line of duty, by all causes (including "felonious" and "accidental" deaths, other than those where COVID was the cause of death). Nationwide, the risk of suicide among police officers is 54 percent greater than among American workers in general[14]. We are losing good men and women, whose collective trauma, never addressed in an effective way, becomes too heavy a burden to carry.

The many layers of new trauma that have come with the pandemic have also had a disproportionate effect on those in law enforcement and other first responder roles. At the start of this book, we cited research on the kinds of traumas that first responders have been exposed to. As staggering as these figures may seem, this data was collected before the events of 2020-2021. As always, it takes time for research to catch up with reality. In the meantime, on January 21, 2022, Michael created a poll that he circulated through LinkedIn, to his first responder network.

---

13   https://datastudio.google.com/u/0/reporting/45630e-fa-3ee8-4c8f-ab44-ccbe743f0b53/page/Kh2dC
14   Sourced 12/8/21 from: https://www.policeforum.org/assets/PreventOffi-cerSuicide.pdf

This is exactly how it was presented:

For first responders only:

How many traumatic incidents have you been exposed to in your professional career thus far?

Nearly 700 first responders replied as follows:

Less than 100 traumatic events	15%
100 to 200 traumatic events	21%
200 to 300 traumatic events	13%
300 to 400+ traumatic events	52%
Total number of responses =	695

It should therefore be no surprise that in the past couple years, we've also seen unprecedented waves of retirements among first responders. To be sure, this is part of a greater trend that some have called "the great resignation." But, in many cases, these retirements represent the collective refusal of many LEOs to continue to work in the system, and within a larger society, that does not support them. Efforts to defund the police mean that these officers are not being replaced.

As the law enforcement ecosystem has shifted, the crimes we're now seeing have become increasingly frequent and progressively brazen.

Across the East Bay, after front porch package thefts, we've seen a second wave of criminal activity – catalytic converters stolen from cars parked on the streets. This kind of theft involves going underneath a car with electric tools and cutting the catalytic converter out of the belly of the car. It's loud and it takes several minutes. But officers are spread too thin to respond in many cases.

Brazen crime that goes unchecked is fuel for more brazen criminal acts.

As we were wrapping up the final chapter of this book, on November 20, 2021, approximately 80 people descended on the downtown Walnut Creek Nordstrom wearing ski masks and holding crowbars. They stormed the store, shattered the glass jewelry cases, and took off in about 25 getaway cars. The police were so under-represented that only three arrests were made. This happened at 8:30 PM in downtown when the streets and nearby restaurants were relatively full of people.[15] Similar flash-mob robberies have happened in several other Bay Area cities –

---

15   ABC News coverage of "Brazen flash mob-style robbery" in Walnut Creek Nordstrom: https://abc7news.com/walnut-creek-nordstrom-looting-robbery-smash-and-grab-wc-broadway-plaza/11260247/

including Pleasanton, Hayward and San Jose.[16] Will this become a new norm for how "holiday gift shopping" is done in the future?

And remember John Davison, Michael's reserve police officer friend, from Chapter 10? A few weeks after the flash mob robbery of Nordstrom in Walnut Creek, John was celebrating his birthday in Carmel-by-the-Sea. On December 7, 2021, while John and his sister perused the goods in a local jewelry store, four individuals in ski masks entered, two carrying sledgehammers, and robbed the store. John and his sister were not physically injured but it was a traumatic experience for both.[17]

These are not isolated incidents, but part of a larger national trend. This is happening in other cities as well - the same trend, in much higher numbers. For example, as of September 2021, the City of Oakland has seen a 100% increase in carjackings and a 50%

16   CBS SF/Bay Area. "UPDATE: Flash Mob Smash-and-Grab Robberies Dampen Holiday Spirit in San Francisco." (Nov 23, 2021) https://sanfrancisco. cbslocal.com/2021/11/23/update-flash-mob-smash-and-grab-robberies-dampen-holiday-spirit-in-san-francisco/ (Sourced 1/8/22)
17   Rosenthal, S. (Dec 7, 2021). KION 5/46 News. "Jewelry store robbed in Carmel-By-The-Sea, one suspect was a minor, DA says." https://kion546.com/news/crime/2021/12/07/jewelry-store-robbed-in-carmel-by-the-sea/ (Sourced 1/4/22)

increase in shootings compared to the same time last year.[18]

We've also seen a dramatic increase in shootings of police officers. According to data gathered by the FBI, as of December 1, 2021, 67 law enforcement officers were "feloniously killed" in 2021, which represents a 55.8 percent increase compared to the 43 officers killed during the same period in 2020.[19]

Michael has his finger on the pulse of greater crime trends, and he convincingly suggests that these trends will get increasingly worse until we collectively remember that the police are a vital part of our society.

In recent years, we've seen a collective shift in perceptions about those in law enforcement roles – from a generally positive perception to one of distrust and disrespect. Something about this shift felt familiar to me. As this writing project progressed, I finally put my finger on it. Perhaps we have done the same thing to our

---

18   "Oakland Police Chief Releases Soaring New Crime Stats, Asks the Public For Help." https://sfist.com/2021/09/03/oakland-police-chief-releases-soaring-new-crime-stats-asks-the-public-for-help/ (sourced 12/8/21)
19   LAW ENFORCEMENT OFFICER DEATHS. 01/01/2021–11/30/2021. https://s3-us-gov-west-1.amazonaws.com/cg-d4b776d0-d898-4153-90c8-8336f86bdfec/LEOKA_INFO.pdf

LEO professionals as we did to our Vietnam veterans? Instead of doing the hard work of weeding out those who abuse their power and looking at the ways we ourselves need to change and grow, perhaps we have designated them as an out-group, to hold and carry our own internal shame. Just as we did with our Vietnam veterans.

If I'm right, why would we do this in theory? Here's why: this gives us an outer focus for our inner turmoil, an emotional scapegoat. It puts a comfortable distance between us and the cancer of racism. It allows us to tell ourselves, "We are not racist. We do not make the wrong judgments about people, out of fear or misunderstanding. It's police who are the real problem. They are the ones who are failing to get it right."

In a way, the echo of respect that we had for police in former days continues, though in a perverse form. While we disrespect them, we somehow see our police officers as having superhuman abilities.

Specifically, we seem to feel that police officers have psychological x-ray vision. In other words, we seem to believe that they can discern peoples' inner motivations while a high-stakes crime is in progress. And we hold police officers accountable, as though they have criminal intent when they have to take a life, even when an armed assailant is rushing at them with deadly intent.

From my perspective, one of the most important insights in this book comes from chapter 3, "Near Death Experience". This chapter shows a collision of two people – Michael, who looked like a drug dealer at the time, and a high school kid with a stolen, loaded weapon. Both felt primally threatened and had very little information to judge each other's motives. Michael broke down after he nearly fired his weapon at this kid. Firing his weapon was the last thing he wanted to do. And when Michael had to take the life of Anthony Banta, he was also devastated.

A driving reason why I wrote this book is to help people understand the heart of first responders and police officers like Michael. At the heart of every good law enforcement officer is the call to be a Protector. They do their human best to judge situations and motivations with the goal of keeping us safe. But the operative word is that they do their HUMAN best. They are not infallible, and they do not have psychological x-ray vision when they make life and death decisions.

And many of them are suffering from years of unaddressed trauma exposure. They are placed in high stakes situations where they see the worst in humanity. Their nervous systems are on continual high alert. Their untreated trauma is dumping adrenaline continually into their systems. Officers are getting killed in the street. Police officers who defend themselves are subjected to being sued and treated like criminals. And yet we expect them to approach each interaction from a neutral stance. No one could do that.

So what can we do to support our first responders?

We need to have their back, in the same way that we support our warfighters.

Specifically, we need to ensure that our first responders have truly safe places where they can directly address their trauma. We need to make sure they have access to trusted Docs and trained peers. We also need to look at treating the biological symptoms that create injuries to their nervous system. Addressing these things will change the entire equation when they are working on the streets.

When our police officers engage suspects, we can avoid many negative outcomes by ensuring that our officers:

1. Engage others from within calm bodies, without fighting a tide of adrenaline in their own nervous system. When our fight or flight system is constantly locked in the "on" position, we are much more likely to filter everything through a perception of threat.

This is where innovative treatments like Stellate Ganglion Block are critical.

2. Have a place to process their own trauma. This will help them see how their own trauma has impacted them and what may trigger them. *What people don't address often controls their behavior.*

3. Have the ability to connect with others, and the emotional intelligence to navigate novel interactions in a grounded, compassionate way. These abilities are the direct result of access to places where these things are modeled and practiced, like the safe peer support circles hosted by the West Coast Post Trauma Retreat.

Finally, we need to do some hard work within ourselves, instead of projecting our thorniest struggles onto groups of people like police officers or Vietnam Veterans. We need to reassess our understanding of the role of Protectors and Defenders, from an empathic stance. We need to see that they are fully human, not superhuman. We need to see that even good-willed people don't always get it right. And that just because a life was taken, it doesn't mean that there was criminal intent on the part of the officer, or that it was the wrong call. We need to reckon with our own moral dilemmas directly. We need to stop pushing our own issues onto other groups of people who are already more burdened than any of us can imagine.

This was Michael's story, but it's not unique. I dedicated more than a year of my life writing *RELENTLESS COURAGE* because I believe it holds insights that will be lifesaving for many who protect and defend us. And because of this, I want Michael to have the last word…here are his final calls to action.

Michael Sugrue's Final Reflections

First, we need to *smash the stigma.* We need to talk about the human impact of trauma. This needs to happen at all levels within first responder professions. For example, for law enforcement, this needs to start at the police academy. Towards the end of training at the academy, we need to bring in people that can talk about the toll of the job. We need to bring in people that will be truthful about the personal impact of law enforcement work. Frankly, we need to expose them to books like this one, stories like this one, and experts like Doc Springer who can put these truths into words with clarity and relevance. If Doc Springer and I can support these kinds of efforts, please reach out to us.

This kind of open communication also needs to happen in field training programs. Field training officers who are assigned to patrol teams need to lead by setting the tone for this kind of sharing. They need to open up about their own experiences or no one else will. When we have a traumatic call, there is time set aside to "debrief". But instead of simply talking about the facts of what happened, we need to move beyond this and acknowledge in words that some of our on-the-job experiences are just really messed up. We need to talk about the trauma that we experience - openly and truthfully.

For example, one of my calls took me to an intersection of two streets where a pedestrian was hit and killed - sandwiched between two high speed vehicles. It was an awful scene. Everybody who responded was impacted by this. We need to be able to say, "you know that was really awful. I felt like I wanted to throw up." We need to talk about and normalize the impact of these kinds of calls.

Second, we need leadership that sets the right tone and consistently supports first responders. We need our leaders to speak from their own experiences and talk about some of their own traumas. During our annual training, we need leaders to open up about the toll of their own careers instead of holding onto a "chief" image. Leadership is about being human, being humble, and being truthful about all aspects of this work.

It is critical that leaders *believe us* when we are impacted by trauma ourselves and *support us* to get the healing that we need. We also need our leaders to hold high standards for hiring. If agencies lower their standards, we will get people into our ranks that should not be police officers. Whatever issues we are having now will become worse in terms of police officer interactions with the public. We need to bring in high-quality people. We need to ensure that those who take the oath are selflessly and fully committed to serving and protecting the public. And we need to pay and support them well so that we can retain the best professionals we have.

Finally, we need to change the relationship we have with the public. We need to bring down our walls and start educating the public in truthful ways about the things we're encountering. We've gone in the opposite direction these past few years. These days, most law-enforcement agencies have a permanent full-time position where a public information officer crafts public messaging. We have seen police departments try to improve relations with the community by shifting from reporting crime after crime, to "feel good stories." There was even an initiative to have police officers lip sync to songs and post this on social media.

What we really need instead of these "fluff" pieces is truthful conversation about the human side of the job. We need to talk about officer suicides. We need to talk about the number of traumatic incidents that police officers are exposed to. This can be done in a way that does not identify specific cases. For example, we might share that last year officers were exposed to 52 child abuse cases, 18 fatal car accidents, 16 child deaths and 18 suicides.

Otherwise, the public has no idea at all. How would they?

We don't share the stories that would help people connect with the human side of the job. To give you an example, there is one rotation that everybody wants to avoid. Every officer is typically assigned this rotation for part of their career. The catchment area is a large retirement community in the East Bay. When you are on this rotation, you might get five or six death calls in a week. The vast majority of the time these are not homicides. They are natural deaths. Still, imagine going out to the scene of five or six deaths in a single week. Often, the bodies have not been found for several days. When you walk into the residence, the body may be bloated, and the smell is hard to put into words – it's unforgettable.

Most people fail to make the connection that police officers and other first responders witness these kinds of things, over and over again. Maybe if they knew some of these truths, they would have a point of connection and a way to find empathy.

Finally, law enforcement needs to really get to know the community that we serve. Proactive policing is very important for keeping the public safe from criminals, but it is also important to understand the disproportionate impact that proactive policing can have on some communities. For example, if someone is struggling to pay their bills and we pull them over and give them an expensive ticket for a missing taillight, how does this impact them and their family? We also need to hear these stories about the human impact of the work we do.

I opened up because I want to tear down the walls between the public and those like me that serve as Protectors and Defenders. I want you to know my heart, and to see my pain. I want you to know that the last thing someone like me wants to do is to take a life. I want you to know how we are impacted by what we do, day in and day out. But we are still your sons and daughters, your brothers and sisters, your fathers and mothers, your uncles and aunts, and part of this greater Tribe we are all part of. We know you are hurting, and we are too, but there is a way for us to find our common humanity and heal each other's pain.

RESOURCES FOR HEALING

CRISIS AND PEER SUPPORT LINES

Emergency Responder Crisis Text Line - Text BADGE to 741741

Lifeline: Call 800.273.TALK (8255)

Crisis Text Line: Law enforcement text BLUE to 741741, others text TALK to 741741

Crisis Text Line - Text BLUE to 741741

Cop2Cop - 1 866-COP-2COP (267-2267)

The following resources are listed in alphabetical order, and those that Michael has personally utilized and found helpful are in bold font. Resources descriptions are taken from each organization's public website.

10-33 FOUNDATION

The 10-33 Foundation is staffed by current and former first responders, military members, and their families who understand firsthand the struggles of living in these career fields. We have compassion for those living this life and our mission is to offer assistance through education and crisis intervention services to provide tools to help them secure healthier lives, marriages, and careers

Website: https://www.1033foundation.org/

Phone: 707-880-0264

911 AT EASE INTERNATIONAL

Provides first responders and their family access to free & confidential trauma-informed counseling, so those who serve our communities can be their best.

Website: 911aei.org

BLUE H.E.L.P.

It is the mission of Blue H.E.L.P. to reduce mental health stigma through education, advocate for benefits for those suffering from post-traumatic stress, acknowledge the service and sacrifice of law enforcement officers we lost to suicide, assist officers in their search for healing, and to bring awareness to suicide and mental health issues.

Website: https://bluehelp.org/

Email: contact@bluehelp.org

BOULDER CREST

Boulder Crest's signature PATHH ("Progressive and Alternative Training for Healing Heroes") programs teach our participants how to make peace with their past, live in the present, and begin planning for their future.

Website: https://bouldercrest.org/

Phone: (540) 554-2727

THE CODE 9 PROJECT

Our mission is to educate, train and advocate for the prevention of PTSD and suicide for all First Responders, Veterans and their families. We come together to help support and save the lives of those weary from saving other's lives. We come together to unite, support and connect our First Responders, Veterans Families, Organizations and Communities for each other's wellbeing.

Website: https://thecode9project.org/

Phone: (929) 244-9911

COPLINE

CopLine has earned the trust of the Law Enforcement community by providing peer listening through a hotline by maintaining complete confidentiality as well as anonymity if the caller chooses. We train competent, confident, committed, and compassionate retired officers to engage with callers on the daily stressors officers and their family members experience.

Website: https://www.copline.org/

Phone: 1-800-COPLINE

FIRST RESPONDER SUPPORT NETWORK

The mission of the First Responder Support Network (FRSN) is to provide educational treatment programs to promote recovery from stress and critical incidents experienced by first responders and their families.

Website: https://www.frsn.org/

Email: info@frsn.org

Phone: (415) 721-9789

FRONTLINE FIRST

Through specialized training, compassion, and faith, we help first responders, military personnel, and the community effectively prepare for, deal with, and reduce the emotional injury caused by crisis and trauma.

Website: https://frontlinefirst.org/

Email: info@frontlinefirst.org

Phone: (916) 259-9987

MIGHTY OAKS

Mighty Oaks provides peer-to-peer resiliency and recovery programs that serve as the catalyst to assist our Nation's Warriors dealing with challenges related to the struggles of daily military life, combat deployments and the symptoms of post-traumatic stress (PTS) offered at no cost to our Nation's Warriors, including travel at beautiful ranches across the US.

Website: https://www.mightyoaksprograms.org/

MISSION 22

Mission 22 is dedicated to healing America's veterans when they need it most — right now. We offer treatment for Post-Traumatic Stress and Traumatic Brain Injury and all of the issues veterans are facing today.

Website: https://mission22.com/

Phone: (503) 908-8505

OSI CANADA (For Canada)

We at OSI-CAN do not see PTSD or Post-Traumatic Stress Disorder as a Disorder, we see it as an Injury you can recover from. If you are suffering from the symptoms of an Occupational or Operational Stress Injury, then a PTSD or PTSI diagnosis is not required to get our help!

Website: https://www.osi-can.ca/

SAFE CALL NOW

Safe Call Now is a confidential, comprehensive, 24-hour crisis line and support service for first responders, emergency services personnel, medical professionals and their family members nationwide. Safe Call Now provides education, support, healthy alternatives and resources to save lives and put families back together.

Website: https://www.safecallnowusa.org/

Phone: 206-459-3020

SAVE-A-WARRIOR

Save-a-Warrior offers an alternative holistic service that equips veterans, military personnel, police, firefighters and other first responders with a community of support and effective techniques to overcome the symptoms and addictions associated with Complex Post-Traumatic Stress.

Website: https://saveawarrior.org/

STELLA (FOR STELLATE GANGLION BLOCK)

STELLA has a nationwide network of clinics that provides cutting edge treatment for Post-Traumatic Stress Symptoms. STELLA is based on the understanding that trauma causes a biological injury, which can be healed with the right treatments and the right support. Stella provides treatments like Stellate Ganglion Block and Ketamine. When STELLA treatments are used in combination with other programs, such as Mission 22's recovery + resiliency program, first responders can achieve long-lasting healing from trauma.

Website: www.stellacenter.com

THE WEST COAST POST-TRAUMA RETREAT (WCPR)

The WCPR program is for first responders whose lives have been affected by their work experience. The WCPR residential program provides an educational experience designed to help current and retired first responders recognize the signs and symptoms of work-related stress including post-traumatic stress disorder (PTSD) in themselves and in others. FRSN prefers to identify PTSD as a post-traumatic stress injury.

Website: https://www.frsn.org/west-coast-post-trauma-retreat.html

Email: info@frsn.org

Phone: (415) 721-9789

THE WOUNDED BLUE

The WOUNDED BLUE offers a national peer advocate support team to provide The Wounded Blue with support, guidance and resources, "Camp Blue," a retreat for injured and disabled officers for peer support and their families, as well as emergency financial aid, mental/emotional health treatment referrals, legal assistance referrals, membership benefits of medical/dental discounts, and access to private anonymous mental health treatment.

Website: https://www.thewoundedblue.org/

RESOURCES FOR FIREFIGHTERS

International Association of Fire Fighters Recovery Center - 866-965-3074

Firefighter Suicide Hotline - 800.273.8255

FIRE/EMS Helpline - 1.888.731.FIRE (3473)

Doc Springer's Website (where photos mentioned in this book and many additional resources are listed) – www.docshaunaspringer.com

About us

Michael Sugrue began his law enforcement career in the United States Air Force as a Security Forces Officer in 1998. As a Security Forces Officer, Michael specialized in Law Enforcement, Global Force Protection, Anti-Terrorism, Nuclear Security, Foreign Air-Field Assessments and Air Base Ground Defense. Michael served in a variety of assignments including Flight Leader, Flight Commander, Senior Watch Officer, Chief of Command Post and Chief of Security Forces.

During his time in the Air Force, Michael served all over the United States, Europe, the Middle East and South America. He was also a Security Forces Phoenix Raven with the unique identifier of #1173. Michael honorably separated from the Air Force as a Captain in 2004.

Immediately after the Air Force, Michael was hired by the Walnut Creek Police Department, where he served in a variety of assignments including Patrol Officer, Driver Training Instructor (EVOC) Field Training Officer (FTO), SIU Detective, Undercover CA DOJ Narcotic Task Force Agent (Contra Costa County), Public Information Officer (PIO) and Patrol Sergeant.

Michael was awarded the Walnut Creek PD Distinguished Service Medal in 2014 for his heroic and lifesaving actions during a Fatal Officer Involved Shooting in 2012.

Michael ultimately medically retired in 2018. He is now a Peer Volunteer at the West Coast Post Trauma Retreat (WCPR) and an Ambassador for Save-A-Warrior (SAW).

Michael is a dedicated advocate for awareness, prevention, education, training on Post Traumatic Stress Injury (PTSI) and First Responder Suicide Prevention. Michael continues to speak at law enforcement agencies all over the United States.

Shauna 'Doc' Springer is a licensed psychologist, best-selling author, frequently requested keynote speaker, award-winning podcast host, and one of the world's leading experts on psychological trauma, military transition, suicide prevention, and close relationships. A Harvard graduate who has become a trusted Doc to our nation's military warfighters and first responders, she navigates diverse cultures with exceptional agility. As Chief Psychologist for STELLA, she advances a new model for treating psychological trauma that combines biological and psychological interventions.

Doc Springer is frequently sourced by the media for her uniquely perceptive insights on trauma recovery, post-traumatic growth, psychological health, and interpersonal relationships, developed from two decades of work at the extremes. Her work has been featured in multiple media outlets, including VICE, NPR, NBC, CNN, CBS Radio, Forbes, Business Insider, Military Times, Military.com, Gun Talk Radio, Coffee or Die Magazine, Havok Journal, THRIVE GLOBAL, US News and World Report, The Daily News, Police1, Anxiety.org, and Psychology Today.

In her book with co-author Jason Roncoroni, *BEYOND THE MILITARY: A Leader's Handbook for Warrior Reintegration*, Doc Springer shines new light on the psychological and relationship challenges associated with military transition. *BEYOND THE MILITARY* asserts that a successful military transition is not ultimately about finding a new job—it is about reconnecting with your deeper identity, enhancing your closest relationships, and discovering the full potential of life after military service. She and Roncoroni provide a detailed, 400-page roadmap to successful transition through this collective work.

In her book, *WARRIOR: How to Support Those Who Protect Us,* Doc Springer takes us into the heart of trauma – how it impacts us, and how we can heal. Her insights, gleaned from working with countless warriors who have overcome extreme traumas, are both critical and timely as we emerge from years of societal trauma. *WARRIOR* has been the focus of collective readings by veteran groups and by thousands of therapists who support service members, veterans and first responders. Doc Springer has also created a virtual online guide that pairs with WARRIOR to deliver her unique perspective and game-changing insights to those who need it – in a confidential, self-paced way, for the benefit of individuals or groups (available at www.docshaunaspringer.com).

Doc Springer offers paid speaking, training, and strategic consultation. To make an inquiry, visit the "CONTACT" page on her website: www.docshaunaspringer.com.